Life's Adventure: Virtual Risk in a Real World

Life's Adventure: Virtual Risk in a Real World

Roger Bate

BUTTERWORTH HEINEMANN

OXFORD AUCKLAND BOSTON JOHANNESBURG MELBOURNE NEW DELHI

Butterworth-Heinemann
Linacre House, Jordan Hill, Oxford OX2 8DP
225 Wildwood Avenue, Woburn, MA 01801-2041
A division of Reed Educational and Professional Publishing Ltd

A member of the Reed Elsevier plc group

First published 2000

British Library Cataloguing in Publication Data
A catalogue record for this book is available from the British Library

Library Of Congress Cataloguing in Publication Data
A catalogue record for this book is available from the Library of Congress

ISBN 0 7506 4679 9

Composition by Genesis Typesetting, Laser Quay, Rochester, Kent
Printed and bound in Great Britain by Biddles Ltd, www.Biddles.co.uk

Contents

Introduction

It seems we live in a dangerous world. Western society is acutely aware of dangers to health and welfare – from infectious diseases and genetic disorders to food poisoning and car crashes. Furthermore, advances in information technology make us ever more aware of these dangers, as the latest scare is spun around the world in a matter of seconds.

Similarly, our society feels guilt and regret for the effects we have on our surroundings – from the climate that makes life possible, to the beautiful creatures we love to observe.

But are we right to fret about the hazards we face and impose on the environment? Of course, we have a responsibility to ourselves and our world to minimize risk, but how far should we take it?

The articles in this book, written over the past seven years, trace my attempts to answer these questions. In my opinion, on the whole, we – and the media and politicians, on our behalf – have overreacted. The articles here, originally published in newspapers and journals, address some of the most important reasons for this overreaction, as I see them. As it is not always possible to discuss contextual issues in opinion editorials, these reasons are outlined in this introduction.

The media – the gatekeepers of ideas and the conduit for scares

There is competition for column inches in all newspapers and there are many more attractive, newsworthy, and perhaps more important, subjects that editors could have addressed every time they used a column of mine. I would like to thank the editors of the *Wall Street Journal, Financial Times, Economic Affairs, The Sunday Times, LM Magazine, Accountancy Magazine, Novo Magazine, Bridge News,* the *San Francisco Examiner* and numerous other papers and web site managers for publishing my articles.

The development of the internet means ever more sources of information are available, yet for the majority traditional sources of information are still vital. Some of these are also significant providers of electronic information – such as BBC Online. Despite the growing diversity of information sources, it is still true that the power to decide what the public should know rests with quite a small number of newspaper publishers, editors and TV and radio producers. For complex issues that involve multidisciplinary scientific input, this power is even more concentrated and one person (for example an environment editor) might determine the particular viewpoint of an entire magazine or even TV Channel.

These 'gatekeepers' not only decide what detail we receive, but through their own language and imagery, they influence what we are likely to remember of these complex issues. Concentration of power, even if it is based in expert knowledge, is rarely a good thing.

How these gatekeepers have changed

In the 1950s writers and broadcasters were, in many respects, simply retailers of science, presenting neatly-packaged information to readers. However, as readers have became more sophisticated and the mood of the times has changed, so journalists have let personal opinion colour their interpretation of science. By the 1960s journalists were discussing the mixed blessings of science, and by the mid-1970s the environmental and consumer movements prompted speculation on the potential risks to human health from new technology. This speculation was further fuelled by several technological disasters: the Bhopal and Seveso chemical spills, the explosion of the space shuttle, *Challenger*, and, of course, the nuclear meltdown at Chernobyl.

Since then, there has been a divergence in public opinion on new technology. Generally, the public views a new medical technology as a good thing – a breakthrough – and is happy to discount drawbacks and reasonably discuss any moral and ethical issues surrounding it. But most other new technologies are scrutinized and criticized for even the smallest environmental or public health threat, the usual public reaction being to fear and resist the change.

Pressure groups need to be sensitive to public attitudes if they want to sway opinions, and of course, the media also respond likewise in publishing the stories they think the public wants to hear and read about. Threats of environmental disasters are newsworthy, but many scientists are dismayed that explosive communications from Green pressure groups are treated uncritically by the media. The *Brent Spar* issue, where Greenpeace duped the media with doctored video coverage, alerted the electronic media to the problems of being spoonfed 'news' by pressure groups. Concerned for their image as much as anything else, the media in the late 1990s are aiming for balance in scientific reporting. But often issues are highly complex, involving scientific uncertainty, confusing statistics and economic trade-offs. It is no surprise that accuracy sometimes becomes hostage to the story, but neither is it acceptable.

Uncertainty, balance and objectivity

Real science is a very laborious painstaking process. Scientific objectivity is achieved by repetitive empirical testing of theories, which are revised in the light of new evidence and/or better theories. Journalists cannot be expected to attain true scientific objectivity, but they should aim for the ideal of neutrality and unbiased reporting by balancing diverse points of view, by presenting all sides fairly, and by maintaining a clear distinction between news reporting and editorial opinion. This ideal is paid lip-service but the media often fail to present a balanced view. Contentious theories and poor-quality research are often given undue prominence; scientific and statistical results are misinterpreted and misunderstood. It happens because of prejudice, time pressure and ignorance.

Balanced reporting by journalists is necessary but not sufficient if the public is to be accurately informed of the science relating to any particular issue. Of course, the ability of journalists to balance a debate requires that they be aware of all relevant opinions. It upsets scientists, who are careful and cautious (the good ones, anyway), that for the media, balance becomes synonymous with objectivity. However, some scientists find comfort in mass support, and are encouraged when they can concur with the consensus of public opinion.

But the popular view is notorious for its wrong-headedness. The American comic, Will Rogers, once made the astute remark that 'we are all ignorant – only on different subjects'. We all hold ill-informed views on subjects which don't closely affect us, and if all our friends think the same thing, we've no incentive to test our views against the evidence. And newsmakers are just as likely to be subject to popular views, they often create them.

Eugenics was very popular earlier this century. It advocated selective breeding (of actual people) to control and improve physical and mental quality. As late as 1986, Singapore enacted a policy of giving pay rises to procreating graduates while bribing non-graduates with housing grants if they submitted to sterilization. Even civilized Sweden had a mass sterilization programme based in eugenics. Hitler of course was the most infamous fan of eugenics.

Other than often being wrong, the main problem with popular theories like eugenics is that they are often poorly discussed. Superficially black or white theories are always grey under the surface, and if a government bases policy on a theory, not supported by good data, its flaws will be worked out in reality and the costs will be borne by real people.

On a smaller scale, but following the same principle, even minor breaches of scientific protocol can be dangerous. Ignoring bias in the peer-review process (Article 2) allowing statistics to be misused in support of a favoured theory (Article 29) and allowing scientific fraud to go unchallenged (Article 24) all delay and deny real knowledge.

What do the media report?

Novelty, singularity, timeliness and human interest are often the criteria which define modern media interest. A highly significant new treatment might pass almost unnoticed by the media, with the beneficiaries finding out from their GP five years later and being none the worse for it. On the other hand, some issue which is not even 'news' but a campaign manufactured by a pressure group to attract attention, could be the most hotly-discussed but least understood and least relevant, 'virtual' risk (Article 29).

Without thinking, we can get very excited about 'low-probability, high-impact' risks. For example, an isolated outbreak of Ebola virus fever in Zaire in 1995 spawned a big-budget Hollywood film which fantasized about the virus spreading to America. Although the fever is horrific, it is unlikely to spread very far because of its short incubation period and high fatality – a really successful virus (like influenza) lies dormant in an outwardly healthy carrier, who can move around freely infecting a large number of people. Besides that, treatment is available, but the film captured the public imagination, tempting the viewer to believe that killer plagues are just around the corner.

Playing on ignorance of genetic manipulation and runaway diseases, the media (supported by certain science interests) make the call that politicians can't resist, 'something must be done', even when that something cannot even be defined. In this way, journalists turn a discussion of public health science, which is not often newsworthy, into public health politics, which is.

Food scares, such as BSE and listeria, have followed similar patterns. The UK ban on beef on the bone, in place from 1997 to 1999, is simply the most egregious example (Article 27). Regardless of the (still debatable) science, the UK government, for fear of being accused of not reacting to concerns about BSE, banned T-bone steaks and ribs, even though it was acknowledged that the risk of contracting Creutzfeldt-Jakob disease from them was 100 times less likely than being struck by lightening.

Missing the story

For the journalist, missing a story is a worse crime than exaggerating one: better to report first; qualify later. There is therefore an inherent bias in favour of alarming the public.

Take the UK birth control pill scares of recent years. In October 1995 the UK Committee on the Safety of Medicines announced in a press release to doctors that certain brands of pill were associated with increased incidents of blood clots. 'Pill Kill' headlines were the inevitable result. The ramifications went beyond selling newspapers; this issue was directly relevant to many women and the effect was a 12 per cent reduction in pill use, and an associated increase in births, abortions and miscarriages.

However, what the papers didn't say was that the risk of blood clots with certain brands was increased from 1 in 100,000 to 2 in 100,000. If women had been given this information, rather than the sensationalist spin, perhaps their personal risk (of a clot) versus risk (of pregnancy) trade-off would have been different and the tragedy behind the statistics could have been avoided.

A few months after this debacle, *The Sunday Times* reported on similar findings in *The Lancet*. This pointed to an increased risk of breast cancer for those on the pill. However, this time there were no alarmist headlines even though the new information was more alarming than that related to blood clots. Much like the short-term reaction after the death of Diana, Princess of Wales, newspaper editors decided to behave responsibly.

I had some involvement in another putative pill scare and I'm pleased to think that I helped to avert a panic (Article 6). A report from the German pill manufacturer, Schering, showed that ethinyloestradiol in the pill had minor reproductive effects on male rainbow trout at very low (0.1 ng/l) levels. I discussed these effects, other naturally-occurring oestrogenic compounds, and the fact that ethynyl estradiol probably didn't even reach rivers. A UK Environment Agency report came out two months later confirming this and playing down the whole scare. The *Sunday Express* (13 October 1996) picked up on my story and ran a slightly alarmist piece, but other than that, the issue died down. Getting all the information out into the open, in a balanced way, left no room for sensation.

Key issues in the battle for ideas

Measurement

One of the great advances in science has been the ability to count, estimate and measure our world. Concentrations of chemicals that were estimated in parts per million (ppm) a decade ago, can now be measured in parts per billion (ppb) or even parts per trillion (ppt). Physics has long worked in numerous orders of magnitude, but now the sciences with more pressing political relevance are following the lead.

Measurements such as kilo (n^3), mega (n^6), giga (n^9), tera (n^{12}), milli (n^{-3}), micro (n^{-6}/ppm), nano (n^{-9}/ppb), pico (n^{-12}/ppt) are seen in the mainstream press, and there are many others, some I know and many I undoubtedly don't. The point is that concentrations of chemicals (say in drinking water or in the air) can now be measured far more precisely than ever before. Trace chemicals in water that could not be measured in the 1960s, and only with massive cost in the 1970s, can now be measured easily.

The existence of certain metals in water can be useful, even essential to our bodies (selenium and zinc for example). However, other metals (such as cadmium and lead) have no known use in the body, and may cause harm in high concentrations. In the past, the ambient concentration of contaminants was often too low to measure, so people did not worry about them. But times have changed, measurement is now possible and concern has followed.

The almost inevitable political consequence of such measurement has been the push to remove all substances known to cause harm at high doses. At first reductions in contaminants were easily made, and improvements in health were obvious, but later reductions have been extremely costly and of dubious benefit. For example, trying to remove the last particles of lead from water so that it is only found in a few parts per billion, costs billions of pounds, with no observable benefit (Article 22). Numerous other articles touch on this theme (Articles 7, 9, 49 and 61).

With our new knowledge of the unseen in our world, we have temporarily lost sight of the rule that 'the dose makes the poison'. Simply because we can measure something in tiny quantities does not mean it will cause harm.

Correlation does not mean causation

Many overweight people drink diet cola, but this does not mean that diet cola causes obesity. We all know enough to dismiss the correlation as spurious, but it isn't always so obvious that an increase in one thing does not *cause* an increase in another. People do not choose to make errors, but there is a tendency to seize upon the first plausible explanation for an unknown effect. As Bertrand Russell caustically observed, if a good reason cannot be found for believing in something, then bad reasons will do just as well. Once we believe in an idea, for either good or bad reasons, we then tend to dismiss contrary evidence.

Several articles discuss instances where correlation is assumed to show cause and effect (Articles 21, 29, 46, 49). Scientific uncertainty is no match for a politician with a plan, and often policy proceeds as though correlation were indeed causation.

Precautionary principle

> Sentence First; Verdict Afterward
>
> The Red Queen, *Alice in Wonderland* (Lewis Carroll).

One of the methods by which a lack of causation does not hinder policy is the precautionary principle. The idea that we should look before we leap is a sound one for individuals, because we are acutely aware of the costs and benefits of personal precaution. We know the risks of driving long distances, but even if the train is safer, it may be less convenient and comfortable than our own car. In short, we trade off safety for time or comfort every day. Of course, if one has the option, not travelling at all is the safest option (at least from transport danger) but then, most accidents occur in the home.

Individuals become frustrated when they feel they have no control over their circumstances and the hazards that they face. Much has been written by journalists and pressure groups about involuntary exposure to the problems of big business or big government (chemical spills, dangerous pharmaceuticals such as thalidomide and BSE for example). However, trying to avert public exposure to risk by restricting people's activities creates another set of problems. The power to restrict actions often resides with a coercive authority, such as a health and safety agency. This power, and the restrictions it leads to, is rarely mentioned in newspapers and journals, but it can create a problem as great as the one it tries to avoid, and I have concentrated on it in my writings. The role of a 'safety' agency is to reduce a particular risk as close as possible to zero. The danger of this one-sided responsibility is that the agency is not required (and may not be allowed) to balance the possible benefits of their actions against the wider implications. For example, safety regulations regarding new drugs make new development extremely expensive and lengthy. This means that only very large companies can afford the research; the resulting drugs will be expensive and will only be developed where there is a large enough market. Prospective patients hoping to benefit from the drug will probably view the risks very differently from the safety agency and may see regulation as a costly nuisance. Furthermore, overall safety may suffer because a risk is displaced from one agency's area of responsibility to another which is not currently under political focus (such as making rail even safer, but making it so expensive that more people travel by car). For more detail and relevance to HSE issues see Articles 31, 34, 41–45, 59, 61.

Consumer activism and public choice economics

Another key problem with public health, safety and environmental agencies is that they benefit from pandering to those most inclined to scare us.

The political landscape has changed recently with the demise of certain democratic processes, such as government committees and government science bodies, and their replacement with other less accountable groups, such as consumer activists, and supranational bodies (see Rabkin and Sheehan (1999) and Furedi (1999) for details).

The economic and political theory that can explain this dynamic is called public choice theory. It explains why institutions and, therefore, the incentives faced by scientists, politicians, pressure groups and businessmen are important to any political process. I have explained this process at length before (see Bate, 1996), but it also appears in many of the attached articles, such as Articles 32–39.

Conventional wisdom says that public servants apply their professional training and expertise in the public interest and not in their own; that government works on behalf of the people for the people. Public choice theorists argue that this view is naive. They examine the individuals involved in the making and executing of public policies and the incentives they face. It turns out that most people, most of the time, find it impossible to argue against their own interests. The bottom line is that bureaucrats, like just about everyone else, respond to the incentives they face and mostly do what they perceive to be best for them and their nearest and dearest.

The public choice model of political decision-making divides society into four groups: voters, politicians, bureaucrats and interest groups (although the latest models include a fifth group – the media). Each group stands to gain something from the system: voters want better government, politicians want votes, bureaucrats want job security and enlarged budgets, interest groups want income. Politicians, bureaucrats and interest groups have distinct advantages over the voters. They are professionals who typically know more about their specialist subject than does the average voter (partly because voters remain rationally ignorant of most policy issues – that is, the benefits of gathering information are expected to be less than the costs). Many social health and environmental issues involve all these groups, vying in a game of competing interests. According to economists Mitchell and Simmons, politicians and public figures:

> find it rational to engage in obfuscation, play-acting, myth-making ritual, the suppression and distortion of information, stimulation of hatred and envy, and the promotion of excessive hopes (Mitchell and Simmons, 1994: 63–64).

One inevitable conclusion from studying the public choice model, is that policies are designed to benefit the professionals in large political systems rather than the voter. In order to curb rent-seeking behaviour, political decisions should be made as close to the voter as possible.

There are numerous examples of where rent-seeking occurs, such as health activists' recent campaigns against smoking. They demand higher and higher tobacco taxes, allegedly to help the poor, who smoke more than the rich. The Exchequer gets enormous revenue (£10 billion in the UK in 1998) but the activists and their attendant bureaucracies guarantee their own existence by acting as quasi-government agencies, being funded from taxation to implement and design anti-smoking action plans (see Article 36).

A second example can be found in the desire of environmentalists to stop international trade in wildlife. They demand policies (encouraged by the bureaucratic elite) that harm the very people and animals they say they want to help (see articles 53–58), whereas with local control of wildlife (including hunting or culling of animals like elephants) the rent-seeking game is short-circuited, and the benefits of trade go to those looking after the animals. Of course, certain issues cannot be dealt with locally, or even nationally. Global warming, or climate change as it has become known, is the prime example. And because the inevitability of an international solution to climate change is so obvious, it is the playground of the world's most astute rent-seekers.

The big lie – climate change is new, due to man and stoppable

Adolf Hitler claimed in *Mein Kampf* that the 'broad mass of a nation will more easily fall victim to a big lie than a small one'. The power of climate propaganda is astonishing – it is the sheer scale of the lie it contains that makes it so enduring. The lie is that we can stop climate change.

As mentioned in numerous articles (see Articles 2, 37, 41, 42, 46 and 47) there is considerable uncertainty as to whether increases in greenhouse gas emissions have caused changes in global temperature (for a comprehensive review see Bate, 1996). But more than this is that somehow mankind is the prime mover in climate alterations. Perhaps after the sun, volcanoes and several other natural occurrences, humans do affect the planet, but we are far from the main mover, let alone shaker (more on that in Article 46). Any climatic influence is more the result of changing land uses than gas emissions. Biologists, chemists, geologists and scientists from many other disciplines find it very hard to believe that carbon dioxide can be such a villain as it is painted (see Article 2). Furthermore, man's contribution to total greenhouse gases is as a drop in a bucket. India and China must be allowed to continue rapid development and will inevitably increase their emissions over the coming years. They know what we in the West have forgotten – that the only thing we can do about extreme weather is to protect ourselves against it, and the richer the better.

The truth is the climate will change regardless of what we do. The scientists working within the greenhouse lobby acknowledge that to stabilize atmospheric concentrations of gases we need to reduce our emissions to less than a sixth of the politically-agreed targets, which is politically impossible. In short, the idea that we can control the planet's climate by tax increases is one big fib.

Combating alarmism and making sensible policies

There is no simple solution either to the degree of misinformation in the public domain or to the process that leads to panic. However, providing more reliable information to the public is likely to help. Science journalists on the whole have done a reasonable job in presenting scientific information to the public. But from a cursory glance at any major newspaper, the column inches devoted to science by science writers is overshadowed by those devoted to environment and health. In the main these subjects which are heavily dependent on scientific information are poorly covered, and usually by non-specialists. Also, the rotation of staff covering these issues appears to be much faster than in the science department. In general, science writers are ex-scientists with science degrees who want to write about science, whereas environment and health reporters are often mainstream journalists who will work on the topic, but could as easily be covering domestic politics, defence or even entertainment. That does not mean they cannot do a good job, just that they will be satisfied with creating the appearance of balance, since they may not have the competence to discern between alleged 'facts'.

So, if mainstream journalists are incapable of presenting relevant facts on an issue, we have a problem. After all, to paraphrase Juvenal, who is to guard the journalist guardians? At the political level, journalists and all forms of writers must ensure that those who decide policy are accountable for their actions. Old imperfect democratic processes are increasingly being replaced, or at least heavily guided, by unelected, single-issue pressure groups. Their power does not have corresponding accountability, and until it does, it will not be properly restrained.

Impacts of Western policies on developing world

The greatest problem of Western activist-driven policy is not that Westerners are deprived of certain products, or that those products are more expensive, or even that Westerners become less safe. The real threat is to developing countries who are often obliged to follow our lead, whether or not the policy is appropriate. Aid is often tied to policies favoured by Western countries, the policies themselves having been championed by single-interest pressure groups (see Articles 3, 48, 49, 52).

As these articles assert, the new battleground for ideas is on the international stage, helped somewhat by the internet and world wide web, and the increasing move towards global governance via UN bodies and international treaties. As Jeremy Rabkin (1999) has explained, the actions of a farmer in Belgium or a public health worker in Tanzania can now be affected by the concerns of an environmentalist in Minneapolis or a health activist in Coventry. It is increasingly important for developing country journalists and politicians to be aware of this process, since the lives of their people are at stake.

Unfortunately, as the article on the Convention on Persistent Organic Pollutants discusses (see Article 52) the elite in less developed countries (LDCs) are being drawn into the process. LDC politicians are just as prone to pressure and rent-seeking as politicians in the North.

Why these articles

Watching the watchdogs is often frustrating, seldom fun, but always interesting. Since I became involved in the policy issues related to science in the early 1990s, scares have proliferated. Perhaps they serve a valuable process, but mostly they seem to be hype to sell newspapers, and indirectly keep watchdog watchers like me employed. It seems that I have a job for as long as the Anxiety Multinationals continue to cause fear and encourage regulatory policy.

Similarity of articles

A problem in publishing a volume of articles that are promoting a set of views is that when writing the articles one has to assume that the audience knows nothing of the topic beforehand. This means that when running several articles in the same book on the same broad theme (such as global warming), there is bound to be overlap. The articles have been edited down to reduce this to a minimum. Therefore, the articles will appear in a slightly revised (usually shorter) version than appeared in print. However, some overlap is inevitable, even desirable, so that the reader can see how history repeats itself (often on the same issue, but perhaps more interestingly on different issues). This happens more often than not because the assumptions made by regulators and others are inherently incorrect (e.g. the political process benefits the voter, individuals cannot make complex decisions, scientists are not subject to incentives). Hence the same problems appear in land management, BSE, global warming, smoking, etc. It is no mere coincidence. Overlap and continuation of similar themes will also demonstrate how the predictions made in the original articles have faired.

The topics, under the heading 'Key issues in the battle for ideas', of measurement, correlation, precaution and activism appear in almost all articles and hence could not provide a means of separation. In an attempt at differentiation, the articles are split into five broad but overlapping topics:

1 Junk science-based scares.
2 How and why scares develop.
3 Regulation and rent-seeking.
4 The new elite – international science bureaucracies.
5 Trade-offs not solutions.

Many of the articles could have fitted into several of the sections, but an attempt has been made to present the similarity in the processes that lead to scares, budgetary allocations or legislation, rather than in topics, such as global warming or pesticides.

References

Bate, Roger (1996). Science under siege: The de-coupling of science from science policy, 7,4 *Energy and Environment*.

Bate, Roger, ed. (1997). *What Risk? Science, Politics and Public Health* (Oxford: Butterworth-Heinemann).

Furedi, Frank (1999). Consuming Democracy (http://www.esef.org/furedi.htm).

Mitchell, William and Simmons, Randy (1994). *Beyond Government* (Boulder Colorado: Westview Press).

Mooney, Lorraine and Bate, Roger, eds. (1999). *Environmental Health: Third World Problems, First World Preoccupations*, (Oxford: Butterworth-Heinemann).

Rabkin, Jeremy and Sheehan, James (1999). *Global Greens Global Governance*, (London: Institute of Economic Affairs).

Acknowledgements

There are numerous people who have helped me over the years. The reason I started writing articles on public policy is largely because of four people, Martin Summers, Fred Smith, Kent Jeffreys and John Blundell, the debt I owe them is enormous. Julian Morris, Matt Ridley, Michael 't Sas Rolfes, Terry Anderson, Jonathan Adler, Robert Whelan, Terence Kealey, Robert Matthews, Frank Furedi and many others whose ideas I have borrowed or who have discussed with me the topics on which I have written here, I thank you. I owe an enormous debt in terms of my understanding of political economy to James Buchanan, Gordon Tullock, Ronald Coase and Douglas North. For my understanding of risk issues I am similarly indebted to John Adams, Mike Thompson, Aaron Wildavsky and especially Bruce Ames. I would like to thank Robert Pollock, Brian Brown, Matt Rees, Mike Gonzalez and Therese Raphael for their help at the *Wall Street Journal*, and Colin Robinson and Anne Colyer at the IEA who helped with all my columns for *Economic Affairs*. But, most of all, I would like to thank Lorraine Mooney, who read all but four of the articles in this book before they were originally published, and who improved my writing from terrible to mediocre.

RB
Cambridge

Part One
Junk Science-based Scares

1 Holes in the ozone theory

Economic Affairs (February 1994)

In a recent *Daily Telegraph* survey, ozone depletion was considered by respondents the 'most important environmental issue facing Britain today', placed above pollution and global warming.

Ozone depletion is a simple, seductive concept – the shield that protects us from the sun is being destroyed by man's activities. The theory was first proposed in 1974, becoming internationally recognized in the 1987 Montreal Protocol, where agreement was reached to halve the use of ozone-destroying chemicals by the year 2000. Environmentalists argue that the Montreal Protocol's precautionary principle should be applied to other, feared yet unproved, environmental issues: to wait and see is not good enough – positive action, based on current knowledge, must be taken now. Dissenting opinions, in the words of Vice-President Gore 'undermine the effort to build a solid base of support for the difficult actions we must soon take'. I agree with the environmental movement that a lesson can be learned from the ozone debate. However, it is not the one they suggest.

Chlorofluorocarbons (CFCs), the alleged ozone destroyers, are non-toxic, non-reactive chemicals first produced by Thomas Midgeley, a Du Pont company chemist, in 1928. He was looking for replacements for ammonia and sulphur dioxide, the toxic and unstable chemicals then used as coolants in refrigerators. Midgeley's discovery eventually created a multi-billion dollar business, reducing the price of refrigerators and providing millions with fresher and cheaper food.

In 1974, however, two scientists, Rowland and Molina, proposed that CFCs from refrigerators, aerosols and solvents could, under the influence of strong ultraviolet light (UV), break up and form chlorine monoxide, which would in turn react with ozone and reduce ozone concentrations.

Ozone is found in greatest quantities between 12 and 70 km above the earth's surface. It is formed and destroyed in a chain reaction catalysed by UV. Ozone thereby reduces the amount of UV reaching the earth. Rowland and Molina alleged that the CFC-induced chlorine monoxide would reduce stratospheric ozone and hence lead to an increase in earthbound UV, potentially leading to more skin cancer.

There appeared to be empirical support for the theory when the 1980s had lower levels of ozone concentration than the 1970s. However, ozone concentrations may be cyclical. Very low levels of ozone were recorded in 1957, well before the mass production of CFCs. Also, CFCs are four times heavier than air, so the concentration of them, even in the lower stratosphere, is only a tenth of that at ground level. Consequently, for CFCs to have caused the recent reductions in ozone, one CFC molecule must have destroyed 10,000 ozone molecules, which is possible but not likely.

How did a theory with several holes in it prompt such rapid international action in the form of the Montreal Protocol? The answer can be found by analysing who gained from CFC abatement.

First, researchers into atmospheric chemistry. In 1992, a US government chief meteorologist, Melvyn Shapiro, commented about the ozone scare:

> What you have to understand is that this is about money . . . If there were no dollars attached to this game, you'd see it played on intellect and integrity. When you say the ozone threat is a scam, you're not only attacking people's scientific integrity, you're going after their pocketbook as well. It's money, purely money.

Second, chemical companies. The price of CFCs went up by 30 per cent after the Montreal Protocol. Was it a coincidence that most of Du Pont's CFC patents had run out? They were making only 2 per cent of their profits from CFCs and they were the leaders in alternative technologies – with high profit margins.

Others who gain are the bureaucrats involved in drafting and monitoring the treaty, and environmental groups whose kudos soared after the treaty was signed. But who loses?

- Consumers in Western countries who will only be able to buy more expensive refrigerators, solvents and aerosols, alleged to be ozone friendly which may not be 'people friendly'.
- Consumers in poor countries, many of whom will not be able to buy the more expensive products and probably will be left to eat less well-protected food.

The lesson we should learn from the Montreal Protocol is that the cost of precipitate action can be very high. However, the lesson that the environmentalists say we have learned is 'act now, or else'. As a leading environmental researcher recently put it, the 'Montreal Protocol [was] merely a dress rehearsal for drastic reductions in carbon dioxide emissions'. Let us make sure that global warming is real and harmful before bowing to environmental special interests again.

2 Is climate change a problem?

Economic Affairs (October 1994)

The 1980s had some of the warmest years so far this century and, coupled with the revival of interest in global warming theory, this led to a panoply of government-funded research programmes designed to estimate the possible problems that might follow. The best estimates of the most-quoted body, the Intergovernmental Panel on Climate Change (IPCC), were that expected increases in carbon dioxide and other greenhouse gases would lead to a warming over the next century of about 2°C. It claimed that there could be potentially serious effects on climate from this warming.

At some time, maybe nineteen months ago, there was a change in the tactics of the greenhouse lobby. Whether it was intentional or occurred spontaneously is unknown to me, but the change occurred nevertheless.

The lobby no longer discusses global warming but 'climate change'. At first I thought the reason was that, like the global cooling proposed in the 1970s, global warming was too explicit. At some stage, if warming does not occur, national governments may become bored with the idea and focus their spending on more obvious threats.

However, the role of carbon dioxide in warming may provide another explanation, a reason that suggests that the switch in discussion to climate change was intentional. A forthcoming paper[1] by Dr Jack Barrett, a chemist at Imperial College, London University, claims 'that any increase in the carbon dioxide content of the atmosphere will not affect the average temperature of the troposphere'. The reason for this is that carbon dioxide only absorbs infrared energy at certain discrete wavelengths. Once these wavelengths are 'saturated', no more warming will occur at those wavelengths. In other words, there is a limit to the warming potentials for all greenhouse gases. Dr Barrett continues:

> All the energy that can be absorbed by the atmosphere is being absorbed under present conditions. Any additional carbon dioxide cannot alter the 100 per cent absorption of terrestrial radiation.

The implication is that carbon dioxide will not be a warming gas in the next century. Other greenhouse gases, such as methane, nitrous oxide and CFCs, can still absorb infrared radiation, but their warming capacity is far less significant than carbon dioxide. Consequently, warming may never occur to any damaging degree. Therefore, the switch from discussions of global warming to discussions of climate change may have been tactical.

But, what sense does it make to suppose that climate change, of itself, is a bad thing which man must try to stop? What real effect can man have on the world's weather – positive or negative? Can carbon dioxide, really be such a villain?

Carbon dioxide is far less important than water vapour as a warming gas and has a beneficial role in promoting vegetation. A group of American botanists have been studying the effects on plants of a doubling of carbon dioxide in their atmosphere. They have produced a fascinating video of their findings, (*The Greening of Planet Earth: The Effects of Carbon Dioxide on the Biosphere*) which shows that crop yields increased and plants required less water to survive in a carbon-dioxide enriched atmosphere. This shouldn't be a surprise, as carbon dioxide is an important input for plant growth. As an old wives' tale says, 'talking to' (or breathing on!) plants makes them grow faster.

Vegetation also has its own cooling effect in preventing the sun from baking the earth.

Carbon dioxide is the only variable over which man has any control, but since total carbon dioxide makes up less than half a per cent of the atmosphere, and the man-made portion is about 4 per cent of that, that control is puny. Without the discovery of fire we would certainly have less carbon dioxide in the atmosphere than we do today, but so what?

The treaty developed at Rio in 1992 concentrated on the stabilization of the atmospheric concentration of carbon dioxide. Yet if the above chemist and botanists are to be believed (and remember they are using empirical evidence rather than model simulations), then the signatories to that treaty are attempting to limit change for no other reason than to prevent it.

That is the ultimate policy for those wishing to control the activities of others, because if we really believe that change is bad, then we would no longer demand proof of damage before accepting policies designed to halt change. This is not paranoid libertarianism. At a recent DOE conference, John Gummer, UK Environment Secretary, declared that climate change *per se* was bad!

1 Global Warning: The Continuing Debate. ESEF (1997).

3 The balance of the ozone debate

The Wall Street Journal Europe (16 August 1995)

Last week's disclosure by scientists in the journal *Nature* that the ozone layer over Antarctica seems to have thinned even further has been followed by demands from scientists and environmentalists for faster phase outs of 'ozone destroying' chemicals. Press reports of third-degree sunburns suffered by the inhabitants of the Falkland Islands have widened support for such radical measures. But is such immediate action needed? Or are the scientists exaggerating their case to gain media attention and garner more research grants?

We might hope that an answer would be provided in the book *How Soon is Now?* (Nicholas Booth, Simon & Schuster, 1994), which is described by its publisher as the first book to give a balanced assessment of the ozone depletion debate. But although painstakingly researched, well written and extremely informative, the book falls short of that target.

Booth provides exhaustive detail on the history of the science of the ozone debate, from the discovery of ozone to the invention of chlorofluorocarbons (CFCs) in 1928 as non-toxic replacements for propane and ammonia as coolants in refrigerators. It was discovered in 1973 that CFCs could break down in the presence of ultraviolet light, releasing a chlorine radical that could destroy ozone in a chain reaction. Ozone, which occurs in a layer many miles above the surface of the globe, is formed and destroyed in a continual reaction in which UV light is the catalyst. This reaction reduces the amount of UV radiation reaching the earth.

Booth self-consciously tries to assume the middle ground between the extreme pronouncements of environmentalists on the one hand, and CFC dependent businesses on the other. But in this debate, as in any other, it isn't ultimately balance but truth that counts.

Evidence supporting the claim that man-made CFCs are destroying the ozone layer, threatening the world's flora and fauna with harmful UV radiation, is shaky at best. The dreaded ozone 'hole' – actually a seasonal thinning – has been detected over the Antarctic ever since scientists started looking, meaning there is no way to know for sure that it isn't a completely natural phenomenon. Much evidence, in fact, suggests that it is. First of all, the 'hole' shows no consistent pattern of growth, becoming larger in some years and smaller in others. More important, ground-based monitoring stations have detected no increase in the amount of UV radiation reaching the earth's surface.

But that hasn't stopped environmentalists from making wild claims. It was alleged, for example, that millions of sheep in the southern hemisphere were going blind due to suddenly increased UV exposure. In fact, the blindness was found to be caused by bacteria, and was actually alleviated by exposure to UV light.

Booth's true sympathies show in his rosy descriptions of ozone scientists. For example, he considers that Gordon Dobson (the man who made ozone measurement possible) was the 'last specimen . . . of the English country gentlemen scientist'. He blames excessive ozone hype on the media, and cryptically states that 'silence must not become the price of objectivity'. He attacks journalists who make apocalyptic pronouncements from scientists' reports, claiming that 'unwittingly, [scientists] have found that their words have been amplified and distorted'.

This exoneration reflects a certain naivety in Mr Booth's work, as scientists respond to incentives like everyone else. They know, as one of them stated, 'if you have a doomsday scenario you get a lot of money'.

While there is no doubt that the scientists involved in the ozone issue have made huge strides in climate knowledge, their opinion on suitable policies is only one of many. Unfortunately, Booth simply ignores or derides the rest. He accepts statements by eminent scientists such as Joe Farman, discoverer of the Antarctic ozone hole, who says, 'We're monkeying around with something we don't fully understand. We must slow production [of CFCs] until we do'.

Similarly, Booth accepts the silly declaration from the former head of the United Nations' Environment Programme, Moustafa Tolba, about the success of the Montreal Protocol to reduce ozone depleting substances: 'Two and a half million people who would have got cancer will be spared'. Yet ozone doesn't even absorb the UVA radiation linked to malignant melanomas.

Increased rates of skin cancer are more likely due to changes in lifestyle (fair skinned people spending inordinate amounts of time in the sun), not ozone depletion.

But the book's most important flaw may be that while Booth is quick to point to the dangers of ozone thinning, he doesn't seem to realize that the abandonment of CFC production has its costs as well. More than just the chemical industry would suffer from CFC abatement. There is, for example, the unquantifiable but certain loss of life in less developed countries that would result if refrigeration technologies became more expensive and thus less accessible. And the chemicals that could substitute for CFCs in air conditioners are toxic and flammable. Failure to recognize such trade-offs is unforgivable in a book so dead set on 'balance'.

4 Are we only half the men we used to be?

The Wall Street Journal Europe (7 May 1996)

As the rust settles on the *Brent Spar* oil platform and the memory of Greenpeace's manipulation of the media fades, environmental alarmists are already back in force. *Our Stolen Future* (Theo Colborn, John Myers and Diane Dumanoski, Little Brown, 1996) was released in Britain last week, after the 25,000-copy first run in the USA sold out within a month. It has already been compared to Rachel Carson's famous *Silent Spring* (Houghton Mifflin, 1962) which warned about the effects of the pesticide DDT on wildlife. In fact, the US National Academy of Sciences has already convened a panel on the issue it highlights and the Environmental Protection Agency is about to announce new regulations in accord with the book's recommendations.

All the concern is about supposedly falling sperm counts and declining fertility, purportedly caused by synthetic chlorine-based chemicals in the environment. The chemicals mimic natural oestrogen hormones and could disrupt human development at critical periods, particularly *in utero*.

Like many environmental activists, the book's authors invoke the precautionary principle. They conclude that these chemicals should be assumed guilty until proven innocent: Since sperm counts are falling we should ban the use of hormone disrupters.

But such a move would be rash considering the study providing the principal evidence for declining sperm counts is seriously flawed. Author Niels Skakkeback did a meta-analysis of sixty-one studies conducted between 1938 and 1990. But some experts say Skakkeback's data from the early years are minimal and haphazardly collected. Evidently, men with low sperm counts were excluded from the early data sets. According to Richard Sherins of the US Genetics and IVF Institute, re-analysis of the data from the best forty-eight of those studies actually reveals a statistically significant increase in sperm concentrations over the past two decades.

The British Medical Research Council's reproductive biology unit also warned recently that male potency was declining so fast that if the trend continued, most men would be infertile by the middle of the next century. But a recent study by Harry Frisch of the Columbia Medical Center in New York shows an increase in sperm counts over the past twenty-five years. Another study by C. Alvin Paulsen of the University of Washington found no decline in sperm counts or semen quality over the same period.

The reason for such disagreement is that analytical techniques and data measurement are so variable. Sperm counts vary with factors like age and duration of abstinence before the sample is provided. It is difficult to ensure identical procedures within experiments. It is an art form to compare one study with another. It is also remarkable how sperm counts seem to vary by geographical location: According to Frisch, New Yorkers are nearly twice as potent as men from Los Angeles.

The authors' strongest specific example of a damaging synthetic hormone disrupter is the case of diethylstilbestrol (DES). Mothers were directly fed high doses of it in hopes of preventing miscarriages. Reproductive effects were supposedly significant, particularly in male offspring. This incident is the primary model for the book's conclusion: 'We are certain of the following: The effects of DES . . . are oestrogenic. Both sons and daughters exposed *in utero* experience . . . reduced fertility'.

But the definitive study on DES, which appeared in the *New England Journal of Medicine*, clearly states that men exposed to DES:

> were nonetheless as fertile as other men . . . Diethylstilbestrol-exposed men had no impairment of sexual function, as indicated, for example, by the frequency of intercourse or reported episodes of decreased libido. Conclusions: High doses of DES did not lead to impairment of fertility or sexual function in adult men who had been exposed to the drug *in utero*.

A chapter by Jonathan Tolman, 'Nature's Hormone Factory' (Mooney and Bate, 1999), puts the whole hormone disrupter issue into perspective. Apparently nature provides a panoply of hormone disrupters. Tolman lists forty-three plants and foods in the human diet that have been shown to be 'oestrogenically active'. The list includes carrots, coffee, garlic, lime, potatoes and wheat. Hardly a rare collection.

After drawing on many medical and veterinarian studies, Tolman concludes that:

> the estimated oestrogenic effects from (naturally occurring oestrogens in food) are 40 million times greater than those from synthetic chemicals, but it is questionable that either is impacting human health.

The authors of *Our Stolen Future* believe that an across-the-board ban is the only fail-safe strategy for ridding the world of hazards still unknown.

However, as the journal *Nature* states in its article 'Masculinity at risk' 'this will not be the first occasion when a presumed link between an environmental contaminant and a risk to health has melted away on close investigation'. Based on such thin evidence, it concludes, it would be self-defeating to push for an outright ban of an oestrogen-disrupting pesticide like DDT when we know for sure that many people are dying from mosquito-transmitted malaria.

Many science researchers will nevertheless be delighted with *Our Stolen Future*. Britain's Medical Research Council recently published a report on male fertility that also conveniently ignored the findings of the *New England Journal of Medicine*. As James Le Fanu, *The Daily Telegraph*'s health columnist, remarked recently:

> The MRC did not include this information – presumably because to do so would make it more difficult to apply for the grants they were seeking to do further research on the matter.

The fact is that *Our Stolen Future* is simply unconvincing because it ignores contradictory scientific evidence and pays no attention to the role of natural hormone disrupters in the environment. It could also suggest banning hot baths and tight underpants, which have also been blamed for declining fertility levels, but presumably that wouldn't justify the wholesale indictment of industrial society that the authors seem to be seeking.

5 Is nothing worse than tobacco?

The Wall Street Journal Europe (26 July 1996)

A recent advertising campaign by Philip Morris likened the risk from inhaling other people's cigarette smoke to that of eating cookies. They wanted to show that the risk of developing cancer from both activities was so small as to be practically meaningless. But because balanced discussions about tobacco have become so taboo, this campaign may have backfired. In addition to angering cookie companies, the campaign also pushed anti-smoking lobbies to demand even tougher legislation on passive smoking, or environmental tobacco smoke (ETS) as it is known to the politically correct.

The campaign, which was withdrawn in France and Belgium recently, partly in response to media criticism, attempts to explain that 'Life is full of risks, but they're not all equal'. To do so, the advertisements list the reported relative risk of contracting cancer from a number of activities, including those beneficial, such as a high-fruit diet, and those harmful, such as a high-fat diet. The figures given are from good scientific sources who can hardly be painted as lackeys of the tobacco industry. The ETS statistic, for example, is provided by the US Environmental Protection Agency.

According to the advertisements and the EPA, the relative risk of contracting cancer from exposure to ETS is 1.19. That is, there is a 19 per cent greater chance of cancer in those who inhale ETS frequently than those who don't. Eating one cookie a day scored 1.49, a 49 per cent increase in risk. A high-fruit diet, by comparison, scores about 0.37, a nearly threefold decrease in risk. A high-fat diet scores over 6, a very significant risk.

But anything less than a relative risk of 2, a 100 per cent risk increase, is considered a 'weak association' and, according to the US National Cancer Institute, 'such increase may be due to chance, statistical bias, or the effects of confounding factors'. The confounding factors for ETS include alcohol consumption and a poor diet, which are linked to exposure to cigarette smoke. Given the practical limits of present research capability, it is nearly impossible to isolate the different factors, and therefore to know whether it is smoke itself or the associated risks that are really the problem. The risks associated with ETS, or for that matter cookie eating, cannot be conclusively assessed. This is the point that Philip Morris really wanted people to understand. But anti-smoking groups have made meaningful debate on the issue nearly impossible.

What appears to have irked the anti-smoking activists most is that Philip Morris used science to promote the freedom of the individual to smoke, and did so in a comparative manner. Nothing, they would like to assert, could be as risky as tobacco. Comparative advertising is banned in some countries and according to Philippe Kaas, managing director of Paris-based OC&C Strategy Consultants 'there's a long tradition of courts ruling against comparative advertising'. But if science is ever to be used in advertising to discuss risk – which by its nature is a relative concept – then comparisons are essential. After all, it is not as if Philip Morris named a particular cookie company. It discussed cookies, which are usually high in fat.

Nevertheless, food companies are especially angered that their product has been associated with risk. They correctly observe that while sound scientific analysis is an essential prerequisite of an informed society, on its own it is not enough. Public reaction to Shell's environmentally sound plans to sink the *Brent Spar* oil platform, or even Britain's mad cow fiasco, show that presenting the best scientific knowledge available coupled with a strong legal case is no longer a sufficient defence for a particular standpoint. Public perception, and in many cases public outrage, have to be acknowledged. Activity risk profiles, as provided by Philip Morris in its advertisements, tell us little about the likely perception of the effects of those activities.

The advertisements also ignore one vital difference between eating cookies and inhaling ETS. The first is necessarily a voluntary risk; the second is sometimes involuntary. Since Philip Morris claims that they are arguing for the right of smokers to choose, they should acknowledge the right of non-smokers to choose to not be exposed to ETS. Whether this means simply continuing to allow non-smokers to choose not to enter smoky places, like pubs, or requires more restrictive legislation, is open for debate. And scientific assessments of relative risks should certainly be part of it.

Given the powerful opponents stacked against Philip Morris, it is not surprising that their campaign came under pressure. What is disconcerting, however, is the way that virtually no one will support the facts that Philip Morris used in the campaign. After all, some of the ingredients in cookies can cause cancer. Then again, so 'can half the chemicals ever tested', according to Bruce Ames, professor of Biochemistry and Molecular Biology at the University of California at Berkeley. Undoubtedly so can ETS, but not at the doses most non-smokers are ever likely to encounter. The public can understand this distinction, but until the media moralists start to respect their intelligence, sound science will continue to give way to alarmist sound bites.

6 Rising fears about falling sperm counts

The Wall Street Journal Europe (10 October 1996)

It's amazing the variety of explanations being bandied about in response to reports that sperm counts are falling. Human physiologists are blaming tight underpants and hot baths, environmentalists are pointing the finger at the wholesale industrial use of organochlorines found in most chemical processes, and new-age Gaian gurus are considering that it was the planet self-regulating 'to stop overpopulation'.

The chemical cocktail designed to halt pregnancy – the contraceptive pill – has so far escaped media scrutiny. But a report to be released shortly by the UK's Environment Agency will show that the active ingredient in the pill, ethynyl estradiol (EE), has been found in samples of river water across Britain and can, even at low concentrations, adversely affect fish fertility. But before the media push people into hysteria with headlines like 'The Pill Can Destroy Your Man's Sperm Count', it should be remembered that more studies are needed to prove a link between EE and falling sperm counts. In fact, there's no proof that sperm counts are falling.

EE can come from other natural and synthetic sources, but overwhelmingly it comes from the pill (via women's urine). Another study from Schering AG, the German pill manufacturer, shows that relatively low concentrations of EE can devastate fish fertility. Although levels of EE in the environment are generally below even these low concentrations, Hermann Schweinfurth, head of occupational toxicology and ecotoxicology at Schering in Berlin, is taking it very seriously.

Journalists seeking sensationalist stories will likely try to link the potential decline in fish fertility and the alleged decline in human fertility. But the bottom line is that the science does not yet support this conclusion. Isolating EE as the synthetic (man-made) cause of a decline in fish fertility may be difficult to achieve, due to the presence of natural oestrogens, oestrone and oestradiol. These hormones probably have a far more significant effect, given that their concentration in the environment is fifty times greater than those of synthetic oestrogens.

Important evidence was recently provided in two chapters by Jonathan Tolman and James Le Fanu[1] for the European Science and Environment Forum. The evidence for declining sperm counts, they conclude, is extremely unreliable: historic sampling mistakes led to abnormally high sperm counts providing the base on which projections were made, thereby giving the impression counts are falling. Also, there appears to be a wide divergence between sperm counts geographically. Finnish men appear to have twice as many sperm as Danes. West Coast Americans have just over half as many as Easterners.

Interestingly, the ambient concentration of most synthetic chemicals were so low as to be overwhelmed by natural chemicals. Synthetics are usually more toxic, pound for pound, than natural chemicals, but their concentration is so much lower than natural chemicals (produced, for example, by plants) that their overall effect is far lower. Environmentalists counter that man has had millennia to adapt to natural chemicals compared with only decades to adapt to synthetics. However, this is dismissed as irrelevant by leading American biochemist, Lois Gold, at the University of California at Berkeley. She argues that 'humans are well protected by defences that are mostly general rather than specific for particular chemicals. In other words, the body defends equally against natural or synthetic compounds'. So, although the toxicity of many synthetics is high, the ambient concentration of most synthetics is tiny and hence their impact is negligible. However, minor reproductive effects occur at concentrations well below those considered toxic to the fish.

Therefore, if we assume for a moment that the concentration of EE is increasing, and having reproductive effects, how should it be handled? And, in particular, how should women react?

An estimated 300,000 women stopped taking the contraceptive pill following a UK government warning last autumn that certain brands could double the risk of thrombosis, or blood clots. The government neglected to stress that the initial risk was so small as to be insignificant, even when doubled, and far less than the risks from pregnancy. Abortions increased in the months following the scare and this summer, births are also up by 25 per cent in many areas from a year ago. William Wilson, the superintendent registrar of births in Birmingham, England, believes the extra workload is a direct result of the pill scare. 'One woman admitted she'd been caught out because she stopped taking the pill, and I expect we'll be seeing more like her in the coming months', he said.

Rational debate must centre around analysis of the data. Given recent environmental scares the data will probably show that little or no action is warranted. If the data are more alarming, then removal of EE at some stage of sewage processing treatment, while developing alternative pill chemicals, is probably the most sensible policy solution. Either way, scaremongers are among us. Both the Environment Agency and Schering would be wise to release all the information they have, in its proper context – or, as a spokesperson for the chemical industry put it, 'another BSE could be on the way'.

1 Mooney, Lorraine and Bate, Roger (1999) *Environmental Health: Third World Problems, First World Preoccupations* (Oxford: Butterworth-Heinemann).

7 The great forest 'rescue'

The Wall Street Journal Europe (11 February 1997)

In the early 1980s Germans worried that their famous Black Forest was dying. Media headlines screamed out: 'The German Forest is on its Deathbed', 'Death Hovers over the Sick Forests'. One newspaper, *Esslinger Zeitung*, even pleaded with its readership: 'Do our pine trees have to die?'

German politicians reacted quickly. Sulphur dioxide from coal-fired power stations was identified as the cause and politicians mandated cuts in sulphur emissions. The rest of Europe soon followed suit to comply with the Long Range Trans-boundary Air Pollution directive from Brussels – that was demanded by Germany. Within a decade sulphur emissions were drastically cut across Europe and the trees started to recover.

It's a neat story that no doubt warms the hearts of those who believe governmental action based on environmentalists' concerns is the environment's only hope. But it's just a story. Some new studies contend that there was no significant problem with Europe's forests in the first place and, even worse, the supposed 'solutions' may have been responsible for some damage. This was difficult to discern at the time given that the issue was driven more by politics than science. And therein lies the lesson for environmentalists and policy makers – precipitating action without all the facts can be counterproductive.

A recent report from the European Forest Institute, a respected environmental think tank in Finland, shows that most European forests have grown on average by over 20 per cent, and some forests by over one-third, in the past few decades. The lead author of the study, Heinrich Spiecker from Frieburg University in Germany, says that the findings are a surprise. He says that five years ago, because of the environmentalists' alarmism, nobody would have believed it. According to the EFI, it is even possible that the increasing atmospheric concentration of carbon dioxide, produced as a by-product of the burning of fossil fuel and blamed for recent global warming, may be aiding forest growth. Carbon dioxide is a necessity for plant photosynthesis and hence growth. The presence of the gas in the atmosphere has risen by over one-third since pre-industrial times.

The EFI report also echoed the German government's Forest Condition Report for 1995, which concluded that the earlier pessimistic prognosis of rapid deforestation was exaggerated. The EFI report contends that in Europe's forests there was a temporary tree 'die-back' in the early 1980s due to drought and pests. And, contrary to environmentalists' claims, sulphur from acid rain was, at most, a minor contributory factor. It is evident from EFI's report that this decline was a blip in an otherwise upward trend in tree growth.

This conclusion, that there is no serious risk to forests from acid rain, is shared in the USA. Ten years ago the US National Acid Precipitation Assessment Program (NAPAP) published a report that shed new light on the green activists' doom and gloom scenarios. NAPAP's multi-million dollar study concluded that no evidence confirms that acidic deposits of sulphur dioxide and nitrogen oxide gases are responsible for the observed changes in American forests. The studies make clear that, as in Europe, the changes that occurred were largely natural in origin.

But if the deforestation in the early 1980s was limited and temporary, then why all the fuss? A brief review of German politics offers some insight. Back in 1982, when the furore began, the German Green Party was interested in abolishing nuclear power; acid rain and forests were low on their agenda. Pro-nuclear conservative politicians, eager to establish their green credentials, blamed the Social Democratic Party for causing *walsterben*, or forest death, by lobbying for government subsidies to sulphur emitting coal-powered stations. It was a vote winner, attracting farmers and forest owners (most forests in Germany are privately owned) as well as urban dwellers.

The Greens, spurred on by the conservatives, successfully mounted an acid rain pressure campaign against the German federal government. The federal environmental agency was interested because it saw a chance to enhance its power in relation to the traditionally stronger *Länder* (the German states). Environmental protection provided the federal government with a policy that allowed for organizational expansion, as well as increased jurisdictional and political influence at home and abroad. It was therefore a compliant ally of the motivated pro-nuclear politicians and Green groups.

According to German energy policy analyst Sonja Boehmer-Christiansen of Britain's University of Hull, sulphur emission control was initially resisted by the industrial sector for fear of higher energy costs, but opposition didn't last once it became clear that the government would act in industry's favour elsewhere. Dr Christiansen says that the German federal government ensured that the German consumer and taxpayer, rather than industry, would pay the clean-up bill. The German government took industry's advice, she says, and lobbied Brussels to force foreign competitors to bear similar environmental cost burdens. The European Commission – never one to miss an opportunity for empire-building – justified the German actions by declaring that limiting these emissions was a means of equalizing competition. This pressure and the discovery of the forest die-back between 1981 and 1984 gave impetus for acid rain abatement policies across the EU.

It took nearly ten years for the anti-sulphur hysteria to die down. This is due in part to other recent studies that have been published on the general effects of sulphur emissions on the environment. First, evidence that sulphur has a stratospheric cooling effect was recently accepted by the United Nations Intergovernmental Panel on Climate Change, in their latest report. Sulphur thereby mitigates up to as much as one-third of alleged man-made warming.

Second, an extensive UK Department of the Environment study in Hampshire showed that rather than dying, Sitka spruce trees actually flourished in an induced sulphur-rich environment, and most trees were not harmed by the significantly elevated sulphur concentration. Elsewhere in England, a sulphur shortage has led to certain crops being sprayed with sulphur compounds.

Third, in Germany, where belief in acid rain abatement remains strong, there is mounting evidence that trees are deficient in sulphur. According to Ewald Schnug, a German academic botanist, sulphur compounds are good at neutralizing ozone, which tends to weaken plants' defences against disease. By adding sulphur to the ground he and his colleagues improved wheat yields by 20 per cent in one year. Mr Schnug concludes that trees are dying from lack of atmospheric sulphur. This information is not meant to take away from the fact that the reduction of sulphur emissions has improved air quality. But what is at issue here is the selective use of data for political purposes.

On balance, as recent reports have outlined, forests are doing quite well. But some researchers are not convinced. Forest growth, they say, may not be all good news: 'My colleagues say that a baby who stuffs himself with chocolate may look healthy, but that doesn't necessarily mean the baby is healthy', says Werner Schumacher, director of the Forest Experiment and Research Institute for the state of Baden-Württemberg in Germany. He suggests that a forest could grow itself to death.

Obviously more research is required. The one thing that is certain about the future of forest politics is that calls for multi-million dollar government intervention for research, regulation and green programmes will continue. But as Europe's experience demonstrates, it's not clear that such programmes are necessary, or productive.

8 Genes, nuts and vaccines

Economic Affairs (March 1997)

Science came alive for me when, as a schoolboy, I read about Crick and Watson's race to discover the structure of life, deoxyribonucleic acid (DNA). I grasped that it was a wonderful discovery, but at the same time I could see no relevance to the wider world.

It is refreshing, therefore, to see geneticists helping to bring improvements to many areas of our lives, from safe blood products to disease-resistant crops to more efficient enzymes in our detergents. All this in less than fifty years. Oddly however, while academic honours for advances in genetic understanding are split evenly between Europe and America, over 90 per cent of the billions of dollars in remuneration are reaped by those on the other side of the Atlantic.

Uncertainty over future regulation often does more damage to business than known, but nevertheless restrictive, regulation. Where there is certainty in the USA there is confusion in Europe. The EU Novel Foods Directive is therefore keenly anticipated by the biotech industry, because current regulations are contradictory and discourage investment.

One problem for the industry is that the Directive is being contested by environmental groups which have voiced concerns about the manipulation of DNA. They have been effective at garnering support from those ignorant of scientific processes but aware of science fiction and the new semantics.

Recombinant, transgenic, gene-splicing, engineering and manipulation are words that conjure up scary images to the layman. European industry, therefore, has an uphill battle compared to the USA, where popular opposition to biotechnology is either lower or less well articulated. Industry's enthusiasm for the EU Novel Foods Directive is consequently dampened by worries that it will restrict the use of genetic manipulation and lead to massive regulatory costs.

The debate over the exact wording of the Directive has hence thrown up two obvious interest groups: pro-use business lobbies, which stand to make small fortunes from the exploitation of new markets, and hence are likely to understate the risks, and anti-use green groups, which, while having a valid ethical message, use alarmist tactics to garner new support and revenues. MEP Gordon Adam is concerned about the role of 'green terrorism' as a key factor hampering public understanding of the issue and sabotaging development of biotechnology.

Caught in the crossfire of the genetic food debate are researchers working in genetically improving pharmaceuticals. A restriction on food research may have knock-on effects for them. Alastair Kent of the European Alliance of Genetic Support Groups agreed: 'Green Groups have been vocal in opposition [to the use of biotech], whereas the users [the patients with genetic disorders he treats] have not been heard until now'.

Genetically modified peanuts may not sell well, and may never attract a sufficient market. But solving potentially fatal peanut allergies may require genetic techniques. A recent breakthrough by Peptide Therapeutics, a rapidly growing Cambridge biotech company, provides a way of blocking the mechanism that triggers the allergic reaction. Dr John Brown, a pharmacologist and finance director of the company, explained that trials had shown the vaccine to be safe and effective. Now, although Peptide's techniques are very advanced they have not used gene-splicing techniques for the nut vaccine. But, according to John Brown, they may want to collaborate with other researchers using these techniques for some of their other vaccine work, on meningitis for example. After the recent deaths of several students from meningitis, a most virulent disease, do we really want to limit this type of biotech research, with the likely breakthroughs it may bring?

Genetically improved foods will lower food costs. Genetically manipulated vaccines will undoubtedly save lives, yet fear of new techniques by 'green' Luddites may hamper further breakthroughs.

Louise Gale of Greenpeace protested at a recent biotech conference in Brussels that biotechnology risked genetic distortion reaching the environment with 'irreversible consequences'. She was joined by three other green groups, which united in demanding a moratorium on genetic manipulation. They all defended their demands with reference to the Treaty of Rome's precautionary principle, which essentially argues that regulators should look before they allow others to leap. They argued that decades of testing are required to prove that there are no risks from genetic manipulation.

The precautionary principle undoubtedly has its place, and ethical considerations should be looked at but a principle of immobility, not precaution, that many environmentalists demand will be very harmful. One only has to look at the faces of the parents of the students killed by meningitis or peanut allergies to count the cost.

9 Pesticides didn't kill Sir James

The Wall Street Journal Europe (5 December 1997)

Under the heading of 'Did big business kill my brother?' *The Sunday Telegraph* (3 August 1997) allowed Mr Edward Goldsmith, editor of *The Ecologist* magazine and brother of the late Sir James, to assert that the chemical industry had caused Sir James's fatal cancer. The truth about chemicals was untold, he claimed, because of a conspiracy of silence perpetrated by companies in collusion with cancer research charities.

While I feel sympathy for Mr Goldsmith for the loss of his brother, that does not excuse the half-baked scaremongering that he is inflicting on an unsuspecting public. His conspiracy theories would be laughably irresponsible if no one listened to them, but regulations based on the selective facts that he and other environmentalists present, would be harmful to our health. Unfortunately, the Danish (and possibly other EU) authorities, may enact such regulations early in 1998.

Mr Goldsmith's most egregious claim is that cancer rates are increasing because of many synthetic carcinogenic chemicals in our food, water and air. However, are cancer rates really increasing?

Cancer is mainly a degenerative disease of the old and rises with life expectancy and better diagnosis. However, with the exceptions of lung cancer, melanomas and non-Hodgkins lymphoma, age-adjusted cancer rates in the United States have dropped 15 per cent since 1950.

While there are undoubtedly synthetic 'carcinogenic' chemicals in our food, the assessment of carcinogenicity is made by tests where rodents are fed chemicals at concentrations often millions of times higher than the equivalent intake of the human diet. Importantly, 'roughly half the natural and synthetic chemicals ever tested are carcinogenic', according to world authority Bruce Ames, Professor of Biochemistry and Molecular Biology at the University of California at Berkeley. For example, orange juice, celery and nutmeg all contain natural carcinogens. Coffee contains over 1000 chemicals and of the 27 tested, 19 are rodent carcinogens. However, as has been known for centuries, the dose multiplied by the toxicity determines the poison. So, although coffee may contain carcinogens, the dose is too low to cause harm.

Interestingly, Ames explains that '99.99 per cent of all pesticides that humans ingest are natural'. In other words, the dose of natural pesticides dwarfs that of synthetics, and yet neither is poisonous in everyday life. There appears to be a threshold dose for most chemicals above which cancer may be caused, but that threshold is almost never breached in the environment, either by natural or synthetic chemicals.

Goldsmith also claims that combinations of synthetic chemicals act synergistically and hence are more potent than the addition of individual chemicals. He cited a recent *Science* magazine article to make his case. However, this article was discredited by numerous experts and was withdrawn by its authors. Furthermore, Ames explains that our bodies' defences against chemicals are 'mostly general rather than specific for particular chemicals' so synthetics have no special potential harm, as environmentalists often claim.

What is particularly worrying is that the Swedish and Danish Environmental Protection Agencies are considering a blanket ban on all pesticides. Policy documents released recently show that they have been swayed by the synergy and carcinogenicity arguments. However, according to Professor Ames these authorities should be far more concerned about diet: 'If reducing synthetic pesticides makes fruits and vegetables more expensive, thereby decreasing consumption, then cancer will be increased, particularly for the poor'. Evidence from America shows that the quarter of the population eating the least fruits and vegetables has double the cancer rate for most types of cancer compared to the quarter eating the most. In other words the removal of pesticides, as Goldsmith demands, would lead to more and earlier cancers.

Environmental pollutants may pose some risk for cancer but they are dwarfed by genetics and diet, the very things that Mr Goldsmith suggests we ignore. His preoccupation with the dangers of synthetic chemicals is misplaced. His desire to banish these chemicals could prove a significant risk to health. Peru learnt this lesson the hard way. In the early 1990s the Peruvian authorities stopped chlorinating their water supplies because of environmentalists' claims that chlorine was carcinogenic. Cholera then flourished in the chlorine-free water, infecting a million and killing 10,000. Synthetic chemicals may pose some risk but it is small compared with the natural hazards around us. The Danish and Swedish authorities would do well to dwell on this fact before enacting damaging legislation.

10 Ban Luddites, not chlorine

The Wall Street Journal Europe (21 July 1998)

There is not much that stirs the lobbying loins of an eco-activist more than industrial uses of organic chlorine. From Rachel Carson's assault on the pesticide DDT in the 1960s to today's attack on polyvinyl chloride (PVC) plastics in toys, chlorine-bashing has never been far away from environmentalist campaigns. And to be sure, elemental chlorine is a caustic gas, a fact I can attest to after inhaling a minuscule quantity in an experimental accident many years ago. But chlorine in compounds is far safer and has saved millions of lives. Unfortunately, recent legislation in Austria and likely legislation in other European Union countries ignores the benefits of chlorine compounds.

How attitudes have changed. Back in 1948 when Paul Müller won the Nobel Prize for his discovery of the pesticide properties of DDT, it was hailed as a miracle. It saved millions of lives by eradicating malaria and typhus from many parts of the world. Indeed, the numerous other inventions based upon chlorine chemistry, including substances like PVC plastics, were then considered to be of huge benefit to society. In the past two decades, the tables have turned on science in general and chlorine in particular. The most recent target is PVC, used in raincoats, plastic bags and children's toys and many other everyday products.

Last week the Austrian government announced that it would ban PVC toys likely to be placed in the mouths of small children. According to government officials, a decree will be issued later this month and measures will come into force before the end of the year. Imports, retailing and advertising of affected products will be prohibited.

Austria's move follows a recent recommendation of the European Commission, which called on EU member states to take regulatory action on PVC toys containing phthalates (chemicals added to PVC to soften it) if they could demonstrate a health risk. The Commission stopped short of accepting the request of Emma Bonino, the Consumer Affairs Commissioner, for an EU-wide ban on PVC phthalates. Austria is the first EU country to put a ban in place. According to one European Parliament member, who wished to remain anonymous, it was done swiftly so that Austria, currently holding the EU presidency, could show leadership on environmental issues. Two other EU countries – Denmark and Sweden – are also on the way to similar bans.

One Greenpeace representative has remarked that 'PVC is a poisonous plastic – replacing phthalates won't solve that problem'. This statement shows that Greenpeace, which has applied much of the pressure for the phthalate ban, is really targeting PVC, and ultimately chlorine.

But, according to a report by the Weinberg Group, a Brussels-based scientific consultancy, phthalates are not harmful at normal doses, and probably not at even vast doses. Professor Christopher Rappe, an adviser to the EU and World Health Organization, considers PVC 'a safe material'. In fact, there is no real evidence that either phthalates or PVC are harmful at all.

Yet Greenpeace has even attacked New Labour's cherished Millennium Dome, saying it must not contain PVC. As usual, it got its way; PVC is being replaced with PTFE (the coating on frying pans). Greenpeace claimed this as a victory, but more than four times as much chlorine is used to produce PTFE as PVC. Furthermore, the original German contractor Koch Hightex is suing the New Millennium Experience company for £3.5 million ($5.7 million) in damages following the change in specification. The British Industry Minister John Battle had to defend the U-turn by explaining that a PTFE-based material would last longer than a PVC-based one, and hence was the sensible choice. But the decision to change was only made after the Greenpeace campaign, and months after the original specifications, leading one to be sceptical of these claims. Like the *Brent Spar* fiasco before it, the taxpayer will again eventually pay for a groundless Greenpeace campaign.

People who care about sound science have to start fighting back. The anti-chlorine activists alarmingly claim that 'It's either chlorine or us'. Chlorine-based products and processes are essential to modern life. Technology-fearing environmentalists are not. The choice should be clear.

11 Farmyard follies

The Wall Street Journal Europe (11–12 September 1998)

This week at a conference in Denmark EU scientists debated whether to recommend banning the routine use of antibiotics for growth promotion in animals. Scientists are concerned that this practice, used to stop early infection in young animals and therefore enhance growth, may induce antibiotic resistance in the animals' bacteria, which may jump species to the humans that eat them. Echoing a similar fear about mad cow disease jumping species, the EU is loath to be seen dithering.

Fears that antibiotic resistance may be increasing are well founded, as tough new strains of salmonella, *E. coli*, gonorrhoea and tuberculosis have recently appeared. Consumer associations, animal welfare and eco-pressure groups, as well as a panoply of regulatory enforcers, have demanded precautionary action. Leading the pack have been Danish and Swedish interests who already operate under a ban on some promoters and want a level playing field. But banning animal growth promoters, as these groups demand, is premature, will be expensive to consumers, and will probably prove counter-productive. In fact, it's just another example of EU countries trying to export the burdensome regulations that they have passed at home.

Bacterial resistance to antibiotics is as old as antibiotics themselves. Bacteria reproduce rapidly and can pass on drug resistance to future generations. New antibiotics are produced to stay one step ahead of resistance to old drugs.

It's also human, and not animal, use of antibiotics that has led to the vast majority of drug resistance. Every time antibiotics are taken for a cold, which is a virus and therefore unaffected, the billions of bacteria in our bodies are given a quick training session in how to resist them, making antibiotics less effective when taken to combat a bacterial illness. And when one fails to complete a course of drugs those germs with slight resistance to the drugs may survive, increasing the likelihood of resistant germs spreading.

Nevertheless, political and media attention has focused on animal use of antibiotics. The UK House of Lords Select Committee on Science and Technology recently recommended that animal growth promoting antibiotics should be phased out. The *New Scientist* magazine explained in a lengthy article that drug resistance came primarily from over-prescription by doctors and dirty hospitals. Yet it concluded that the UK should follow the Danish and Swedish lead and ban animal growth promoters immediately.

But in July the EU's Scientific Committee for Animal Nutrition largely condemned the Danish ban. It called the data presented by the Danish government in favour of a ban 'misleading' and 'speculative'. It concluded that the use of the virginiamycin growth promoter did 'not constitute an immediate risk to public health'.

Furthermore, the twelve-year-old Swedish ban has recently been attacked by an influential insider. Berndt Thafevelin, recently retired head of the Swedish Animal Health Service, claims the ban has backfired. Zinc oxide was added in huge doses as a replacement for the growth promoters. Dr Thafevelin says the zinc was less effective in suppressing disease, as more antibiotics were subsequently used to deal with outbreaks of infection, and has led to environmentally damaging zinc contamination of manure.

The costs have been significant as well. For example, the Swedish policies pushed up farmers' costs to $1650 per sow, making them uncompetitive with their EU partners. They, like the Danish pig farmers, have been squealing for a level playing field. But, according to the animal health division of Pfizer pharmaceuticals, the costs of an EU-wide ban would be significant, reaching as much as $2.5 billion per year for producers and consumers. These costs would threaten the export potential of all poultry, pig and cattle farmers in Europe. How long after that would it be before an EU-wide ban on imports of produce from countries that still used promoters?

Large veterinary drug companies and farmers make easy scapegoats and soft targets, especially for governments that need be seen to act for the public health. But the situation is really not that bad. The age of antibiotics may end some day, but there are antibacterial chemicals we have barely begun to develop. And genetically manipulated vaccines are on the horizon for killers like meningitis.

The Swedish experiment should be a warning to those contemplating banning antibiotic promoters across the EU at Friday's Copenhagen conference. Such bans are unwarranted on the evidence so far available and could even backfire by encouraging a black market in them. As one farmer told me, farm incomes are at an all time low at the moment, and a further dive in profits caused by a drug ban may lead some desperate farmers to buy growth promoters from whatever source they can, undermining the proposed legislation.

12 What's in a name? Emotional words obscure facts

San Francisco Examiner (24 October 1999)

Would you allow this product in your house? It is highly explosive. It is the proven cause of several deaths every year. Countless more are seriously injured. You must depend on regulators and the suppliers of this product for its safety and efficacy. If they make a mistake, you and your family could die.

No way, you say? Well, it's natural gas, which for decades has heated millions of homes around the world. It allowed us to quit burning coal, which created urban air so dark and dank that tall buildings were invisible a few streets away and lung disease ran rampant.

What do you think of this one? Farmers are adopting carbon-based biological technologies to make novel foods to be sold at premium prices in niche markets. Some proponents are demanding government subsidies to expand their technology. However, evidence shows that these food products decay rapidly and may lead to a far greater chance of certain types of food poisoning. Dr Dennis Avery of the Hudson Institute, using US Centers for Disease Control data, found that individuals who eat foods produced with carbon-based biological techniques are eight times more likely to contract the potential fatal strain of *E. coli* bacteria that killed hundreds in the USA in 1998 and left thousands with permanent organ damage. These food products carry fewer (if any) label warnings than are required for conventional products.

A recent survey carried out by my colleagues found that 81 per cent of people, when told those facts, felt the government should warn consumers about the dangers of this technology, and 65 per cent felt it should be heavily regulated or possibly banned.

Never heard of carbon-based biological technology? It's organic farming, given a more precise name to illustrate a point: If you deny people all the facts, they will reach conclusions based on emotion.

People who support organic and natural farming do so under the belief that it produces the safest, purest foods possible. But the facts listed above are just that – facts. In the USA, organic food represents only 1 per cent of the food market, but in 1996 it accounted for 8 per cent of *E. coli* deaths. The bacteria can be transferred through the use of animal manure.

OK, so you were misled. I gave you facts disguised under another name. But how about the people who are going around Europe in moon suits and gas masks ripping up biotechnology test plots and calling for a ban on 'Frankenstein foods?' Do you think there might be any misrepresentation there?

These people have no facts to make their case against genetically modified foods, just vivid imaginations and a talent for fear mongering. These activists who oppose GM foods imagine problems that do not exist and will probably never exist. Biotechnology is rigorously tested, more so than any other method of producing food. It is much more precise than traditional crossbreeding. Scientists isolate the one gene they want to exploit, and they test it.

Activists also do not tell of the many benefits of biotechnology, such as reduced dependence on chemical insecticides, the ability to produce greater yields and more nutritious foods.

Biotechnology is the best hope we have of being able to meet the global food demand, which is expected to nearly double in the next thirty to forty years. For example, the insertion of new genes has increased the yield of Chinese rice hybrids by 20 to 40 per cent.

Current forms of high-tech agriculture, which fed the last doubling of the population, cannot do it again, and organic agriculture absolutely cannot do it. Unless we want to plough up more land currently set aside for wildlife, we need to do something different and we need to do it soon.

Lucky for us, the benefits of natural gas were recognized decades ago, before the age of the eco-warrior.

13 Chernobyl's real victims

Published on various websites in 1998

In the decade since the Chernobyl nuclear catastrophe thousands of people have died and hundreds of thousands of births have been affected by its fallout. But the deaths are due to radiophobia, which caused extensive political fallout, and not from radiation-induced illness. According to UN scientists looking at the medical effects of Chernobyl, the real disaster has been psychosomatic disorders that were manifested by the mass media hysteria at the time. This hysteria encouraged inappropriate government actions in the former Soviet Union such as forced evacuations from locations that might have been contaminated with radiation.

The nuclear core meltdown that occurred at Chernobyl in the Soviet Union in April 1986 was a tragedy for the hundreds of people actually working at the plant. Of these about one third (134 people) were diagnosed with acute radiation sickness, and 28 of these died within the first four months of the accident. Since then a further 17 of the patients who survived the acute phase have died. These later deaths were caused by lung gangrene, sarcoma, and non-radiation diseases or accidents. For their families Chernobyl was a disaster, but for many others it didn't have to be.

Partly because the international media were denied access to the site, but also because of the acute radiophobia that has gripped Western thought since the Second World War atomic bombing of Japan, Western media assumed the worst. *The Daily Mail* on 29 April 1986 filled half its front page with the words '2000 DEAD'. They further claimed that the dead were not buried in cemeteries but at 'Pirogovo in the radioactive wastes depository'.

The next day, *The New York Post* claimed that 15,000 bodies had been bulldozed into nuclear waste pits. Later the Natural Resources Defence Council claimed there would be 110,000 post-Chernobyl cancers in Central Europe and Scandinavia. Several years later on 13 October 1995 Reuters announced that '800,000 children were hit by Chernobyl, as in a nuclear attack'. Over the following months, the BBC, Greenpeace and the numerous European dailies joined the bandwagon to claim that tens of thousands were dead or dying because of radiation.

According to Professor Zbiegniew Jaworowski, a medical adviser to the UN on the effects of radiation 'perhaps the most important factor in creating the Chernobyl mythology was the assumption that any radiation dose, even one close to zero, has some detrimental effect'. This assumption, on which the world's regulations are based, is called the linear no-threshold hypothesis (LNT). This means that there is no threshold below which the effects of radiation, which are observed at high doses, cease to appear.

This hypothesis contradicts all experimental and epidemiological evidence, which demonstrates no harm (and even some benefit) at low radiation doses. Our bodies can obviously deal with a low level of exposure to radiation, and it may even stimulate our systems' defences and make us healthier. The LNT hypothesis is like assuming that one should fear a temperature of 25° Centigrade because at 250° Centigrade one would receive potentially fatal burns. There are numerous places on the planet (Norway, Iran and even Cornwall) where natural radiation is far higher than occurred within a few miles from Chernobyl after the meltdown, with no known human harm.

Following the accident there was a small increase in radiation levels in Russia, the Ukraine and Belarus. Massive radiation screening programmes were established in these regions and in other countries such as Poland, and incidence of thyroid cancers (the form of cancer most likely following acute exposure to radiation) had not increased over a ten-year period. Indeed the Brestoblast region of Belarus, the area with the second lowest radiation level, had the highest incidence of thyroid cancer.

According to Professor Gunnar Walinder, a Swedish radiobiologist, the LNT hypothesis, and not radiation, is the real health hazard. The belief that any exposure may be harmful leads to disproportionate policies to remove people from this hypothetical danger.

Furthermore, nearly 5 million people in the former Soviet Union have been affected by severe psychological stress, leading to psychosomatic diseases. The main stress was inflicted on those living in areas where the media and government informed them that it was fatally dangerous to live. Forced evacuations of the 850,000 newly categorized 'Chernobyl victims' was planned. In the end, 400,000 people were forced to move. Many of these people suffered from gastrointestinal, endocrinological and other non-radiation induced problems. Relocation occurred for over five years, causing the destruction of family and community social networks, and according to Jaworowski 'exposed the relocated persons to resentment and ostracism in the new localities, where old inhabitants treated them as privileged intruders'. Relocation started with those exposed to most radiation (levels about the sixth the background level in Iran), but soon people exposed to doses of radiation lower than in Cornwall were being moved.

Among those moved, morbidity and mortality rates were far higher than those who stayed behind. And the cost of the process ran into billions of dollars. One estimate endorsed by Jaworowski puts the cost to Belarus at $86 billion. Perhaps saddest of all is that as many as 200,000 abortions were conducted of 'wanted' pregnancies in order to avoid non-existent radiation damage to the foetus.

Apportioning blame between the media and the Supreme Soviet is a difficult task. But undoubtedly, unfounded Western fears based on the linear no-threshold hypothesis encouraged the mass evacuation programme undertaken by the Soviet authorities.

Chernobyl was the worst possible meltdown of a poorly designed, constructed and managed nuclear reactor, with the release of significant quantities of radionuclides into the atmosphere. Yet, according to the UN Committee on the Effects of Atomic Radiation, the death toll from the accident itself and directly related effects is thirty-one. There were no early death cases among the public. Apart from an increase in thyroid cancer registry (probably due to increased screening rather than a real increase in incidence) there is no evidence of a major public health impact related to the ionizing radiation twelve years after the accident. No increase of overall cancer incidence or mortality that could be associated with radiation exposure have been observed. The real deaths from Chernobyl were induced by poor policies based on outdated scientific understanding. And yet today the LNT hypothesis still forms the basis of radiation thinking. It is a bizarre indictment of the anti-nuclear world we inhabit.

14 The retreat from scientific reason

The Financial Times (23 November 1999)

Would you deny your child a much-needed medical drip if you were told that the plastic tubing might give your child cancer? Probably not. But the European Commission's decision last week to ban certain plastics may be the first step towards denying patients the best drip materials.

The ban on phthalate plasticisers used in soft toys for those under three years is not justified by scientific evidence and it confirms the power of the green lobby over the Brussels bureaucracy. Even the head of the EU Scientific Committee on Toxicity, Eco-Toxicity and the Environment, Professor James Bridges of the University of Surrey, says the emergency ban is unjustified. 'It's a bit of a surprise to see an emergency action being taken on phthalates' he continued.

Phthalates are chemicals added to hard plastic like PVC to soften it so that it can be more widely used for things like medical tubing, rubber gloves, plastic bags, raincoats and soft plastic toys, such as rubber ducks and teething rings. Phthalates have been used for over forty years in all manner of plastics and have improved life considerably for all medical patients, and provided hours of fun for millions of children, including me. No ill effect has ever been noted.

But phthalates are comparable to a coating material found on the surface of plastics like PVC, and as such over time can migrate from the PVC to the surrounding environment, which could include blood products or children's saliva. Furthermore, phthalates are carcinogenic to rats. On the basis of these two points, Greenpeace and other green pressure groups have demanded a ban, calling phthalates 'toxic' and painting pictures of imminent problems for children and patients the world over.

But their case is horribly flawed. First, the amount of phthalate that will migrate from toys or medical products is tiny. Second, tumours found in test rats resulted from massive doses – thousands of times higher than the maximum dose a child is ever likely to receive, even chewing a teething ring ten hours a days for life. Even the EC accepts that findings on rats 'may have little relevance for humans'. What it neglected to say was that about half of all chemicals (including natural ones) ever tested cause cancer in rats – largely because of the dosage used. Such tests provide some scientific information, but basing policy on them is unsound. On this criterion orange juice, nutmeg and broccoli should all be banned because of the natural carcinogens they contain.

Furthermore, the independent American Council on Science and Health (ACSH) convened an expert review panel last year to address public concern over the potential health hazards of phthalates. The group conducted an exhaustive review of the plastic softeners to determine whether humans were at increased health risk from exposure to these compounds. Members consulted primary and secondary scientific literature, risk assessments published by regulators in America, Canada and Europe, and scientific manuscripts still in preparation, to ensure the findings contained the most recent research. The report's chairman, former US Surgeon General Dr Everett Koop, said 'consumers can be confident that vinyl toys and medical devices are safe'. We should all 'breathe easy. And don't go out and throw all your toys away' concluded Dr Koop.

The case for a ban is further undermined by Bill Durodié, a fellow of the European Science and Environment Forum and author of *Poisonous Dummies* (July 1999), a paper published by ESEF on the phthalates scare. He says that the EC has studiously ignored evidence of human consumption of phthalates from food. According to Durodié's findings, most evidence shows that we absorb higher doses of phthalates from food with no ill effect, than from toys or medical devices. Perhaps in an attempt to avoid another food scare the EC has ignored this data.

In a partial climb down, a spokeswoman for Consumer Affairs Commissioner David Byrne, claimed that the Commission had only used the word 'emergency' because they were required to by the EC's General Product Safety Directive. In addition, she pointed out that no EC staff believed the ban 'a serious emergency'. She also considered that the EC was frequently blamed for not acting quickly on public concern.

So, under pressure from media and public concern (inspired and driven by anxiety pressure groups) products that have been used since the 1950s with no known harm, are to be banned with immediate effect. But this is just the beginning. Greenpeace say the EC has not gone far enough. They want bans on phthalates in medical products.

But phthalates have been used for up to 5 billion patient days of acute exposure and at least 1 billion patient days of chronic exposure without incident. The ACSH report says that the main phthalate 'used in medical devices, is not harmful to humans even under chronic or higher-than-average conditions of exposure. DEHP [phthalate] confers considerable benefits to certain medical devices and procedures, and its elimination without a suitable substitute could pose a significant health risk to some individuals'.

The Greenpeace campaign to ban medical uses of phthalates must not be allowed to succeed. It would be illogical, counter-productive, expensive and a retreat from scientific reason. But then so was the ban on phthalates in toys. We live in strange times.

Part Two

How and Why Scares Develop

15 A new religion?

Economic Affairs (April 1993)

Since the time when primitive men still huddled in caves earth worship has been at the centre of pagan ritual. In the absence of scientific knowledge it was easy to imagine earthquakes and volcanoes as the handiwork of gods. All cultures derive from this common past and the vestiges of paganism are rarely far beneath the surface. However, never before has such a faith pervaded a secular democracy as thoroughly as environmentalism – modern man's earth worship – has today.

Behind the mass of well-meaning people who just want a clean environment lie the committed deep ecologists, the evangelists of environmentalism. The Norwegian Arne Naess who coined the phrase 'deep ecology' advocates returning to medieval lifestyles, 'humanely' reducing the size of the world's population and abandoning science. He believes that 'people can then oppose nuclear power without having to read thick books and without knowing the myriad facts that are used in newspapers and periodicals'.

Some deep ecologists believe that plants and animals have intrinsic rights comparable to man. As the high priests of environmentalism it is only correct that they act in proxy for the unspoken rights of the world's flora and fauna. These deep ecologists see the need for a significant social and cultural transformation. According to environmental writer Lewis Mumford, 'nothing less than a profound reorientation of our vaunted technological way of life will save this planet from becoming a lifeless desert'.

The deep ecologists' most controversial tenet is that humans should not disturb nature. This anti-humanism is at odds with traditional Judeo-Christian values as expressed in Genesis 1:28: 'Be fruitful and multiply; fill the Earth and subdue it. Have dominion over all the animals on the earth'. It is as important for a true deep ecologist to be anti-human as it is for them to care about the environment. John Todd, an environmental biologist, unearthed a technique to mix toxic sludge with microbes that metabolise the sludge and produce clean potable water. Rather than praising his ingenuity at discovering such a useful process the deep ecologists shunned him and many of his environmentalist friends no longer talk to him. Why? He had discovered a solution to an industrial problem and hence taken away an argument against economic growth.

Thus, the main thrust of the deep ecologist position is anti-capitalist. The theological argument against growth markets and technology is epitomized by the author of *Small is Beautiful* (Vintage, 1993), the late E.F. Schumacher. He believed that free markets 'take the sacredness out of life, because there can be nothing sacred in something that has a price'. For example it is considered morally repugnant to trade in ivory, even though those countries which do so have increasing elephant populations. Countries such as Kenya which promote views similar to Schumacher's have seen their elephant populations halved in recent years. Continuing in this vein, the environmentalists, Jonathan Porritt and David Warner, express their distaste for industrial societies.

> The danger lies not only in the odd maverick polluting factory, industry, or technology, but in the fundamental nature of our economic systems. It is industrialism itself – a super-ideology embraced by socialist countries as well as by the capitalist West – which threatens us.

As in most pagan religions the deep ecologists rely on apocalyptic predictions and the occasional catastrophe to buttress their position.

Catastrophes are rare, but when The *Exxon Valdez* fouled the rocky shores of Prince William Sound in Alaska, the deep ecologists showed the influence they have over politicians. The three billion dollars that Exxon must pay will be a penance for sins against nature. The costs of the measures undertaken will vastly outweigh any identifiable benefits.

What the environmentalists ignore is that the ability to protect the environment is enhanced, not hindered, by wealth. 'Industrialisation is the only hope for the poor' as the socialist C.P. Snow acknowledged. There are indeed a number of similarities between socialism and the new enviro-communists. Deep ecology, like socialism, requires central control and an aversion to private property. However, at least the old-style socialists were aware of the importance of wealth, and even claimed to like people.

All of this would be interesting but unimportant if it were not for the militant aspect of modern environmentalists. It is not enough that the adherents worship the earth, the rest of us must bow down before Gaia as well. We must not assume that ardent environmentalists are just on the fringe of society, or within small lobbying groups. The World Bank's Herman Daly has argued that 'Christian theism has done much to bring about the dangerous situation to which the world has come'. He considers 'the rise of this vision [deep ecology] . . . has been one of the greatest advances of this generation'.

If the deep ecologists succeed in their objectives we will hurtle down a green road to serfdom, providing an unhealthy, unsafe and thoroughly unpleasant place in which to live. However, if we can see environmental problems, such as pollution, for what they are – a nuisance – we then can, and will, provide economic and legal remedies and grow sustainably.

16 Coase's lighthouse

Economic Affairs (June 1993)

A general problem with academic disciplines is that poor theories, propounded by influential thinkers, often go unchallenged. Depending on the eminence of the author, this can continue for some time (see *Statistical Snake-Oil*, Robert

Matthews, Feb. 1999, see www.esef.org). It takes a brave man to overturn an orthodoxy, but one such was economist Ronald Coase, later rewarded with the Nobel Prize. He demonstrated that empirical testing of theories is the surest way to assess their worth.

Until Coase's paper 'The Lighthouse in Economics' appeared in 1974 (Coase, Ronald (1974). 'The Lighthouse in Economies' *Journal of Law and Economics*, **17**(2), October, pp. 357–376) it was assumed that lighthouses had always been provided by the state due to the impossibility of securing payment from the owners of the ships that benefit from the existence of the lighthouse, making it unprofitable for any private individual, or firm to build and maintain a lighthouse. Coase was dissatisfied with this traditional analysis offered by famous economists, such as Arthur Pigou, J.S. Mill and Paul Samuelson, among others, and examined the history of British lighthouses for himself.

He found that, in fact, there were lengthy periods of the seventeenth century when no public lighthouses were built at all in England and Wales, although 'at least ten (private lighthouses) were built by individuals'. Their keepers could charge a levy at the local ports to cover their costs and profits. Coase found that not only were there men, to quote Samuelson, 'odd enough to try to make a fortune running a lighthouse business', but they were actually succeeding in doing so. The government's only role in this system was limited 'to the establishment and enforcement of property rights in the lighthouse'. In other words, lighthouse owners could enjoin non-payers through the courts.

However, pressure from the British shipping industry for lighthouse levies to be paid by general taxation were successful, and by 1842 private lighthouses no longer existed.

Coase had exposed a general lack of appreciation for the role of private property rights in lighthouses. A similar lack of vision exists in applying the concept of external cost – the backbone of much environmental and health economics. One overused example is the paper mill located on the banks of a river which releases effluent into the water at no cost to itself. The costs of the resulting pollution are borne by the downstream users. This external effect constitutes a market failure that should, it is explained, be corrected by government. Regulating the effluent level or taxing per unit of effluent are the usually proposed solutions.

The basis of this externality example is that it is assumed that there are no well-defined rights to the water. As no one owns the water, no one has the incentive to stop it being polluted and hence any pollution goes unpunished, without action from a benign third party – government.

But all British landowners whose land backs on to a river have the right to have water passing by in its natural state of purity. This right, known as a 'riparian right', is enforceable under Common Law, and the actions of nuisance and trespass are available to obtain damages and injunctions against polluters.

In essence, the landowners do not have the right to the water itself (they must not appreciably diminish the flow by abstraction or direct more water for personal use than is deemed 'reasonable' by the courts), but they do have the right that the water remains in its pure state.

Rivers are rarely, nowadays, used as a direct drinking water supply, and it is difficult to see the landowner valuing the water highly as the only obvious benefit of pure water is its clarity and lack of odour. Therefore, pursuing an action against a polluter is unlikely, as he may lose the case and has little to gain from winning it.

However, anglers may value the water quality very highly as a medium for fish, as only good quality water will support such sensitive species as salmon and trout. They are therefore more likely to bring an action than a landowner who does not use the water directly, especially as the anglers may buy the right to fish in his stretch of the river. Even so, one still has to prove both the source of the pollution and material damage to the fish in the river.

It was because of these risks that 1948 saw the foundation of the Anglers Co-operative Association (ACA), a body designed to fight pollution on behalf of the angling clubs in England and Wales.

The clubs pay a membership fee to the ACA which indemnifies them against the legal costs of bringing an action under Common Law, following a pollution incident.

The ACA advises the angling clubs to obtain a lease from the riparian owner, so that the clubs have a proprietary interest, which is needed for any Common Law action. Without a lease, the riparian owner would be required to bring the claim because a verbal agreement or a licence does not constitute a proprietary interest.

Since its formation, the ACA has amassed over 17,500 members. They have brought 2000 actions, of which they have lost only one. Some of them have been benchmark cases, and have obtained hundreds of thousands of pounds in damages. Apparently very few polluters pollute the same stretch of water more than once. It seems that Common Law action acts as a good deterrent; its threat is credible.

In conclusion, pollution from paper mills will not be costless if anglers use the river, because of the damages the mill owner will have to pay to the fishing club. Hence, pollution of rivers need not cause external costs if the right over the water is established and exercised in the form of fishing rights.

Before we accept the conventional economic analysis and assume that individuals cannot protect the environment, we should investigate what they do, as Coase did, rather than what economists, politicians and environmentalists think they do.

17 Balance and counterbalance

Economic Affairs (Summer 1995)

Recent press coverage of three environmental books by Wilfred Beckerman, Richard D. North and Matt Ridley have highlighted the lack of balance in environmental reporting. In almost every review of these books a representative of an environmental pressure group was consulted to give an opinion. Balanced journalism indeed. But Beckerman, North or Ridley – in my opinion the country's leading environmental commentators – are never consulted when the latest Greenpeace paper is released.

To provide a counter-opinion is extremely important. If no alternative is given, the original pronouncements remain unchallenged, often leading to more extreme, insupportable statements which again remain unchallenged.

Alleged man-made climate change is a case in point. Recent predictions by the Intergovernmental Panel on Climate Change (IPCC) – the scientific body whose role is to advise the negotiators of the Climate Convention – claim that increasing atmospheric levels of carbon dioxide will lead to rising average global temperatures. However, as mentioned in a previous column (*Economic Affairs*, **14**, October 1994, Article 2 in this book), Dr Jack Barrett of Imperial College, London, contests this, contending that carbon dioxide cannot absorb any more infrared radiation and hence lead to warming. His research was published at the end of March in the journal *Spectrochimica Acta*.

Barrett alleges that Sir John Houghton (head of the Scientific Working Group of the IPCC and Chairman of the UK's Royal Commission on Environmental Pollution) attempted to interfere with the publication of his paper by writing to the editor of *Spectrochimica Acta* in December last year. From the letter, Houghton appeared to have been under the impression that Dr Barrett's paper was already in print and that, therefore, he was not interfering with the process. But it must have been obvious from the copy he saw, which had no date or page and volume numbering, that it had yet to be published. He argues that Barrett's chemistry is 'wrong', but as Barrett commented, 'I am confident in what I have written in the paper'. Since the paper has been through extensive peer review, he does not stand alone in holding a counter-opinion.

That members of the IPCC might resort to censorship is of little surprise. The IPCC has recently been heavily criticized by scientists and politicians for breaking its own rules of procedure, for excluding opinions that do not conform to the consensus and for having work peer reviewed by those who subscribe to it.

The desire for unanimity is easy to appreciate: politicians want a simple story to convince their constituents of the need for urgent action and scientists want funding, which is easier to obtain if an obvious political return can be demonstrated. Consequently, a consensus vision is eagerly supplied by the IPCC.

Those from within the IPCC network such as Dr Philip Jones of the Climate Research Unit at the University of East Anglia tend to believe the IPCC consensus regarding carbon dioxide and global warming rather than Barrett's personal view. But history is littered with widely accepted incorrect science stories, such as the earth was flat, the sun orbited the earth and, more recently (in the 1970s), that dangerous global cooling, not warming, was imminent.

Science is not conducted by committee and truth is not decided by majority voting. It should be as open and objective as possible, and if this means acknowledging uncertainty then so be it. Dr Barrett hopes his paper will:

> promote a thorough scientific examination on the basis of the climate models and will lead to results which are accept[ed] by the whole scientific community and will not mislead governments and industries into premature and potentially economically imprudent decisions.

The counterbalance provided by him and other bold scientists will be a step in the right direction. Whether journalists care to report their findings will be another matter.

18 Lessons from *Brent Spar*

Economic Affairs (Winter 1995)

Now that the waves have subsided and the rig rots in a Norwegian fjord (destined possibly to pollute the coastline), it is time to assess the effects of this sorry incident. Aside from the serious topic of decommissioning redundant oil platforms, it is instructive to assess the roles played by science and politics in governing the actions of Shell and Greenpeace, the two central protagonists.

Shell's conservative public relations effort assumed that, as long as the company was reasonably open with its scientific information and complied with government requirements on decommissioning, environmental activists would be satisfied. Unfortunately for them, Greenpeace's selective use of science (subsequently proven incorrect) stirred up the emotions of European middle-class Greens.

The boycott of Shell service stations in Germany, and the bombing of the stations by eco-terrorists, gave Europe's largest company an enormous environmental credibility problem. But it might have been able to overcome this had other issues dominated the public eye. A North Sea Conference at the time provided Greens with receptive political ears. Political capital was easily gained by condemning Britain.

The stone throwers ignored the fact that more pollutants than contained on the *Brent Spar* flow from the mouth of the Rhine every twenty minutes, and argued that to dump a rig into the marine commons was morally wrong.

Political leaders were prepared to argue, much as Greenpeace had done, using data like a lawyer might to make a case, rather than as a scientist should, to discover what is the case; science plays a limited role in Green politics.

Having said that, enacting policy where there is scientific consensus to buttress a decision is easier in the absence of conflict. Consequently, politicians require, and bureaucrats attempt to provide, a consensus of scientific opinion. However, demanding agreement at the cutting edge of research is profoundly unscientific and may even stifle scientific progress. The most obvious example of this phenomenon is data provision and analysis of global warming. The Intergovernmental Panel on Climate Change (IPCC), the body which advises governments on global warming, proudly claims a consensus among its 120 contributing authors, and 230 reviewers from 130 countries. Consensus among so many? Or acquiescence among the majority?

Whilst protecting their research grants and maybe their jobs, these climate scientists play into the hands of environmental lobbyists. This is because funding hinges not just on consensus but on 'bounded uncertainty'. As Dr Boehmer-Christiansen, a leading science policy analyst, puts it, 'Too much certainty undermines the need for diagnostic research, too little risks losing policy relevance, political friends, and research grants'. In turn this leads to policy being made without direct reference to the science. The cry, 'something should be done', has been formalized as a principle and dignified with a name – the precautionary principle.

Adopting the precautionary principle negates any contribution that scientific judgement can make to policy, for it means that, given *any* theoretical possibility of harm, such as from global warming, no matter how great the uncertainty in the theory, action must be taken to prevent harm.

Professor Fritz Böttcher of the Global Institute of Natural Resources in The Hague, cites an example of potential precautionary principle folly. In response to the recent 'near miss by asteroid' scare, the US Congress commissioned NASA to assess the risk of a direct hit. Ladbrokes would have given enormous odds and gleefully taken bets, NASA, on the other hand, convened two expert panels, on detection and interception, proposed a twenty-five-year investigation and building at least six new ground-based telescopes. On the agenda of the interception panel was discussion of 'deploying a nuclear armada of missiles to deflect a doomsday asteroid from its path'. This, in the name of precaution.

Professor John Carey of the University of Oxford, recently said that 'the effect of discrediting science has been to allow ignorance to appear not merely excusable but righteous'. This anti-science rhetoric is a boon to the environmental movement. Is it any wonder that Greenpeace is selective in its use of science? It is to its advantage to be inconsistent. Policy, made without science or judgement under the precautionary principle, is grist to the extremist mill. That is the lesson from the *Brent Spar* farce.

19 The search for safety

Economic Affairs (Summer 1996)

Whilst environmental lobbyists agree that we have always been exposed to risk, many think that the cultures and priorities of modern industrial societies are leading to a continuous intensification of risks for everyone, not just the wretched poor.

As the BSE episode has shown, there is a fundamental misunderstanding amongst the British public and media about risks and what science can deliver. The public wants to know that a product is safe and scientists are pressed for the answer. But scientific method is not about proving theories (proof is impossible to attain) but about refuting old ones and replacing them with better ones. Scientists therefore cannot claim that something is safe – there is always a risk attached. For example, compounds in coffee are carcinogenic. However, scientists can often estimate the relative risk of consuming one substance compared with another, and put that risk in the context of everyday activity.

Dangers have become more apparent to modern society. As analysis becomes more sophisticated we discover new things, some of which are disturbing. Science has provided the ability to detect, isolate and test the effects of myriad chemicals, whether man-made or naturally occurring, on laboratory animals. The problem comes when a culprit is sought for unknown events, the fashion being to focus on man's activity. There is money, power and kudos in altering public policy. Man's power over nature is small, but his power over other men is significant. Anthropogenic change can be halted, unlike most of nature's. Man's activities are therefore more stringently analysed than nature's.

The fashionable scare in the USA concerns falling sperm counts and declining fertility, alleged to be caused by exposure to synthetic chlorine-based chemicals (known as hormone disrupters). According to the precautionary principle, chemicals should be assumed guilty until proven innocent: since sperm counts are falling we should ban the use of hormone disrupters just in case they reduce fertility. But apparently nature provides a panoply of hormone disrupters. Many foods in the human diet have been shown to be oestrogenically active, including carrots, coffee, garlic, lime, potatoes and wheat, for starters. Hardly a rare collection.

There is a vast array of plant chemicals that disrupt animal reproduction. Probably the most famous is clover. In Australia in the 1940s fewer and fewer lambs were being born. Ewes were becoming sterile and by the middle of the decade sheep ranching in Australia was in a state of crisis. It was discovered (although it took several years for the compounds to be identified) that the clover the sheep were feeding on contained disrupters.

After drawing on many medical and veterinarian studies, hormone expert, Jonathan Tolman concludes that 'the estimated oestrogenic effects from [naturally occurring oestrogens in food] are 40 million times greater than those from synthetic chemicals, but it is questionable that either is impacting human health' (see Tolman in *Environmental Health: Third World Problems; First World Preoccupations*, eds Mooney and Bate, 1999).

But because man has made synthetic disrupters, these have become the culprits. It is a case of finding an interesting phenomenon (lower sperm counts), making it out to be potentially dangerous by extrapolating from a short-term trend and then targeting a human cause, whether guilty or not.

It is the equivalent of the ducking pond for witches. An untoward event occurs, a woman is denounced as a witch. If she drowns she is innocent (and another is sought); if she survives, she is a witch and must be burned at the stake. Hormone disrupters will be called to account for numerous ills – falling IQs and sperm counts are just the first. They are ubiquitous and will be seen to be iniquitous and ripe for banishment.

Scientists must learn to defend themselves in this new political climate, and to be successful they must retain scientific integrity and use the media wisely, being proactive and not just responding to the latest scare. Until that happens each exaggerated story benefits the regulator and the environmentalist and harms science and the taxpayer.

20 Shell shouldn't bow to environmentalists

Wall Street Journal Europe (5 June 1996)

Last month, Shell, the Anglo–Dutch oil company, won a significant battle against several environmental organizations when the UK Advertising Standards Authority, a government advertising regulator, agreed that these groups had misled the public about Shell's activities in Nigeria. Yet, at its annual general meeting and on two television documentaries, Shell was treated with disdain by the press. Scandal-driven journalists were interested in only one story: Shell Nigeria committing environmental and social destruction. In fact, it looks increasingly like Shell may have been the victim of widespread sabotage.

Shell has been operating in Nigeria for over thirty-five years, but it was not until 1990 that its polluting activities became newsworthy. The spark was the struggle of the Ogoni people, a minority group whose traditional lands had been used for oil drilling. Initially, the Ogoni's agitation for self-government led by the writer Ken Saro-Wiwa, who was later executed by the Nigerian government, was driven more by politics than pollution. But few foreigners were interested in questions of ethnic discrimination between Africans or the brutality of a military regime. Environmental despoilation was a different matter, all the more so because it involved a multinational oil company. The tribe's pleas for restitution were taken up by environmentally concerned groups and companies such as Greenpeace, Friends of the Earth and The Body Shop.

In 1995, these organizations paid for full-page advertisements in UK national newspapers showing a gas flare, with the headline 'Dear Shell, This is the Truth and it Stinks'. The impression given was that the picture had recently been taken in Ogoniland. Shell complained that the photo was three years old and that the advertisement incorrectly implied that the company still operated in Ogoniland. In fact, Shell pulled out in April 1993 because of threats to employees. The UK Advertising Standards Authority backed the oil company on both claims. An unrepentant Greenpeace spokesman said, 'The issue is not what the advert said, but what is happening in Nigeria and Ogoniland'. Regardless of Greenpeace's loose use of the truth, there is undoubtedly pollution in the delta. But what are the underlying causes, and is Shell to blame?

An independent British environmental researcher (who wishes to remain anonymous) who has worked in Africa for decades, and in Nigeria since the late 1980s, claims, as have many local Ogoni leaders, that the National Youth Council of Ogoni People, set up by Saro-Wiwa, 'deliberately caused pollution to enhance their compensation claims and to gain international visibility'. It is also alleged that NYCOP used wooden levers to break open the pipeline joints to give the impression of leaking pipes. It is telling that 90 per cent of all pipelines in Ogoniland were damaged, compared with 30 per cent in the rest of the oil-rich delta, despite the fact that sabotage for compensation was also common in other areas.

Brian Anderson, head of Shell Nigeria, recently said that, 'throughout the delta you are looking at people who have little option other than what we have to offer and so you are going to hear stories of inadequate compensation [for environmental damage] . . .'. Shell claims that in 1995 50 per cent of its leaks were caused by sabotage. Compensation claims follow from every discovered leak. Shell also claims that in the past it was unable to clean up pollution in the delta, whether caused by poor maintenance or sabotage, because of NYCOP's threats to its personnel.

Given the apparent sabotage as well as the Nigerian government's scorched earth policy in Ogoniland (an attempt to militarily crush Ogoni resistance), it is unfair to single out Shell for despoiling Ogoniland. Furthermore, Agip, the Italian oil group, which no one has complained about, houses the Government's military police. Why have the greens not gone after Agip?

The demands from Western environmental groups that Shell should pull out of Nigeria persist, but they are misplaced and naive. In fact, the Nigerian economy and the environment are likely to benefit from Shell's presence.

Given that oil is the largest export from this populous and poor country, it seems inevitable that with or without Shell the oil pumps will keep going. Add to this the fact that confidence in the Nigerian military regime is very low, resulting in a very low rate of foreign investment in Nigeria, and the prospects for the environment do not look good. Overseas investment brings new technology and higher standards of environmental protection, even if those standards are not as high as those in the investors' home country. Nigeria's elite have already removed their own liquid assets from the country. Further capital flight by Shell would only accelerate further this downward spiral in confidence.

Moreover, as Brian Anderson points out, even if Shell removed all its 300 expatriate employees from Nigeria, there would still be '5000 Nigerians who are very capable of producing the oil [so] there is no way that oil fields would shut if we took our people out'.

The problem for Shell is no longer local but global. Shell seems to be incapable of taking a stand on any environment-related issue. It caved in to Greenpeace over the disposal of the *Brent Spar* oil platform, it didn't criticize the Nigerian government enough over the kangaroo court proceedings that resulted in the hanging of the Ogoni's leader, Ken Saro-Wiwa, and it buried reports from its own environmental experts on the state of pollution in the delta. In fact, it has angered all participants in every recent debate. At a meeting last month one shareholder commented that Shell was 'adopting a policy of blowing in the wind'.

Shell had an enviable international reputation and it has probably the best operating standards of all the companies in Nigeria yet it seems determined to give the impression of cowering to the demands of green groups and of hiding information. It's easy to sympathize with Shell when every environmental organization, and most journalists, delight in attacking it, but cowardly behaviour only invites further bullying.

21 Damp, but not doomsday

Sunday Times (5 February 1995)

With much of lowland Europe under water last week, there has been a rush among scientists and environmentalists to speculate that man-made global warming is to blame. Is there any evidence for this?

Big floods have occurred throughout history. In 1663 Samuel Pepys wrote in his diary that 'there was last night the greatest tide that ever was remembered in England, all Whitehall having been drowned'.

More recently, the great floods of 1953, caused by exceptional tides, washed over southern England, driving seawater miles inland. This disaster sparked the parliamentary discussions that led to the construction of the Thames barrier.

In 1989, when global warming fever was at its height, Bryn Jones, then director of Ark, the environmental activists, predicted that Grimsby and Great Yarmouth would become permanently flooded by the middle of the next century. Last week's warnings were more circumspect, but most saw climate change as a factor.

Professor John Harries, of Imperial College, noted that warmer winters, higher rainfall and increased frequency of natural disaster are 'not inconsistent with man-made climate change'. He also agreed, however, that other natural phenomena, such as the ocean-warming El Niño effect, volcanic activity or some other unknown natural variability, may be to blame.

Sir Crispin Tickell, the government's sustainable development adviser, emphasized that 'there is an accumulation of evidence' that climate change is occurring.

In this he is at one with Greenpeace. Its recent report, *Climate Time-Bomb* (1994), cites 500 examples of big climatic events, suggesting man-made climate change is responsible. Jonathan Porritt, the former director of Friends of the Earth, says this is 'just one part of the global warming jigsaw'.

Is it? Dr Wessels, of the Dutch meteorological office, believes man's activities have heightened the chance of flooding, not through the emission of 'greenhouse gases', but due to infrastructural changes. He explained that 'exceptional rainfall levels, not seen since 1926, coupled with full aquifers, and the impact of narrowing the Rhine [to help the barge transport industry] means that flooding is more likely'. Man has contributed to the floods, but not through emissions.

Brian Hoskins, Professor of Meteorology at Reading University, is even more forthright: 'There is no evidence that the past fortnight's rainfall and flooding is correlated with global warming'.

The reality is that linkages of natural phenomena with alleged man-made climate change reflect a cultural desire for knowledge about dangerous events and our ability to control them.

Pandering to this desire has been the job of science salesmen. As Dr Roy Spencer of NASA observes: 'It is easier to get funding if you can show evidence of impending climate disasters. Sure, science benefits from scary scenarios'.

Pop culture has always been attracted to catastrophes and has warmed to (and been implicitly voted for, through the political system) scientists presenting apocalyptic visions. Everyday access to dramatic statements has been readily supplied with the advent of supercomputers. Given that there are so many potential climatic variables, it is child's play to find a record broken on any particular date. How about 'the wettest 5 February in Wetherby since records began'?

We cannot yet know that climatic disasters are becoming worse and more frequent. All we know is that we are spending more time measuring and therefore discovering them.

It is quite possible that man-made global warming increased the severity of last week's floods. It is possible, too, that the El Niño effect or volcanic activity was partly to blame. Much more likely, however, is that the flooding of lowland Europe was a natural phenomenon. To infer anything about man-made global warming from the week's events is wishful thinking.

22 A clean water proposal that muddies the issue

Wall Street Journal Europe (6 February 1995)

European Union countries could be facing an estimated $85 billion bill to reduce lead in drinking water if a proposal from the European Commission is approved by the Council of Ministers and the European Parliament. It's hard to be against cleaner water. But the Commission's proposal, however well intentioned, overlooks the potentially serious economic consequences of legislation that is unlikely to have any tangible benefits.

The Commission's proposal, which would modify the Drinking Water Directive adopted in 1980, envisages reducing the allowable concentration of lead in drinking water to 10 micrograms per litre from 50 micrograms per litre. Another part of the Commission's proposed changes would modify the pesticide requirements.

The costs of the proposed lead changes are dependent on the softness, or corrosiveness, of the water in any location. The softer the water, the easier it is for lead to leach into it. Since most lead is leached out by soft water as it sits stationary in household pipes, changing these pipes would be the most sensible way to reduce the lead content in water.

The European Commission puts the cost of changing all household piping – which would be required to comply with the directive's objectives – at $65 billion. France, Britain and Italy would, according to the Commission, bear the highest costs. But recognizing that these costs would be unpopular (as much as $24 billion in France), the Commission declared that member states would only be legally required to change their street piping – household pipes could be left alone.

While this means that EU countries will not be paying out billions of dollars to comply with an unnecessary directive, governments could still be spending a lot of money for no good reason. According to the Commission, replacing street piping could cost as much as $20 billion. But such a move would have virtually no impact on reducing the amount of lead found in tap water (water in street piping is rarely stationary and therefore lead does not have the opportunity to leach into it).

In other words, the chief objective of the legislation – cleaner water – is unlikely to be achieved, though EU countries will be asked to cough up $20 billion or more to give the appearance of complying with the drinking water directive.

This is all rather ironic since the main impetus for the Commission's new proposal is the high level of non-compliance with the 1980 drinking water directive. Non-compliance has stemmed from an array of factors, but mostly it has been a recognition on the part of national governments that meeting the commission's standards on water quality would involve a severe, and unnecessary, disruption in countless industries, such as agriculture (the Common Agricultural Policy implicitly encourages the use of pesticides and nitrate fertilizers).

Nonetheless, the effects of non-compliance have been insignificant. Take nitrates for example. One of the motivating forces for a reduction in water-nitrate concentration was the fear of its impact on infant mortality – the so-called 'blue-baby syndrome'. But in Britain, there has been only one reported case of this syndrome – and no deaths – in the last 20 years, even though target nitrate levels have regularly been breached.

This highlights the key problem with the Commission's proposed changes: It is predicated on questionable science. Most scientists agree that lead is a dangerous neurotoxin capable of stunting childhood development at high blood levels, but there is disagreement about the threshold at which those effects begin. All substances, even water, can be poisons, but it is the concentration or dose of that substance that determines this fact, not merely its existence.

Much of the concern over lead stems from a famous 1979 study by Herbert Needleman of the University of Pittsburgh. The study purported to show that children with relatively high, but non-toxic levels of lead in their blood (250 micrograms per litre) had demonstrably lower IQs than their less-exposed peers. More recently, and one of the stimuli for the Commission's new proposal on water quality, the World Health Organisation has reaffirmed the link between reduction in IQ and blood lead levels – but at concentrations higher than found by Needleman.

The validity of the Needleman study has been called into question, and a thorough analysis of it is now impossible as the author claims to have lost his raw data. However, even if we take the Needleman and WHO studies at face value, the impact of lead on IQ pales in significance compared with other factors. Marjorie Smith, a British paediatric expert, has stated that 'moderate elevations in body lead burden play only a minor role, if any, in determining a child's IQ when compared with parental and socio-economic factors'. Given that reducing lead levels in water will have high costs and, hence, deleterious socio-economic effects, it's questionable whether the Commission proposal is warranted.

There are also problems with the pesticide part of the drinking-water directive. The Commission's proposed changes include scrapping the long-standing requirement that the ambient water concentrations of combined pesticides should be no more than 0.5 micrograms per litre. Unfortunately, however, they are still insisting on individual pesticide concentrations of less than 0.1 micrograms per litre.

John Finney of Zeneca Agrochemicals highlights the absurdity: 'Drinking 13.5 gallons of water is equivalent to eating one apple, as far as pesticides are concerned. Actually implementing this directive may mean that 60 per cent of pesticides will be scrapped'. The British Environment Secretary, John Gummer, has noted that 'this standard is much more stringent than is necessary on health grounds for most pesticides now in use'. While pesticides are often condemned by environmentalists as posing a health risk, the reality is that pesticide use ensures a better quality, and a higher quantity, of food. The normal use of pesticides does not pose health hazards.

What seems to have been missing from the Commission's proposal was any risk analysis. As the late regulatory expert, Aaron Wildavsky pointed out, 'ultimate safety' is an impossible goal, but one can choose to take the safer path between a number of options. However, this safer path is likely to involve the acceptance of new risks.

Despite this logic, there are those who can gain through the directive's implementation. Water companies will benefit from stricter legislation because they will be allowed to increase the price of the water they sell to their customers and increase their staff levels to comply with the new regulations. Similarly, environmental groups who demanded action will push for the proposed changes to be adopted, and the Brussels bureaucracy will benefit by having more work to dole out.

In the end, the big loser will be consumers, who will have to pay more for their water with no noticeable benefits in return. Indeed, the real effect of the directive is likely to be higher government spending, higher taxes and, in turn, a reduction in social welfare.

23 Post-environmentalism

Economic Affairs (Autumn 1995)

The war of ideas fought between socialists and *laissez faire* adherents swung decisively to the latter with the demise of the socialist states in the late 1980s. The intellectual battleground has shifted. The Left has retreated and regrouped into its heartland: the social provision of health and education, and more recently, the environment. Green issues were readily adopted by the Left in the early 1980s and became a central tenet in the early 1990s.

In many ways the environmental movement was more useful to those who still believed in command and control than either health or education. It had broad support from all age and socio-economic groups. Although many of its members realized that the capitalist system with limited government provided the best answers for the economy, they firmly believed that only government could provide the answers to environmental problems. Most importantly, it had, as Eric Heffer explained in *The True Believer* (Perennial Library, 1989), the best of all unifying agents – hatred. 'Mass movements can rise and spread without belief in a God, but never without belief in a devil'. The environmental movement had found a ready scapegoat (destined never to be an endangered species!) which unified the Left – big business. Self interest and the search for profit are considered not only amoral but lead to uncontrolled pollution, with the citizens picking up the tab.

It is claimed that big business, through its powerful lobbying, has stopped legislation that would protect our environment and that it is polluting our rivers and air with little remorse and even less compensation. To combat this desecration, so the popular conception goes, new Left-green anti-business alliances have sprung up to force through legislation.

The reality is somewhat different. By the time legislation has been negotiated and enacted, lobbying special interests from all sides have had their say. The one certain thing is that the winner is never the consumer and their environment.

However, the really clever move of the command and controllers is their switch from national to international concerns. The legitimacy of national government is observably in decline. In economic terms alone, huge budget deficits, increasing taxation and ballooning sovereign debts highlight governments' lack of authority.

Politicians and bureaucrats, correctly assessing that respect for them has all but vanished at home, seek admiration and income from new impressive international posts. Compared to the strictures of producing national legislation, with the entrenched special interests involved and the voluminous existing statute book, the international arena is a virtual *tabula rasa*.

Politicians of all creeds clamour about the latest overseas environmental problem: international protest carries more *kudos* than local action and avoids home pressure groups and business lobbies. Also, once a treaty is ratified, those bureaucrats who fought so hard for it can blame it for all the ills that follow.

Most damaging is that, while domestic governments come and go, an international convention and its accompanying institutions are never transient and always costly. The worldwide ban on ozone depleting substances enshrined in the 1987 Montreal Protocol costs Western society over $100 billion per annum, with a greater price paid by those in Third World countries who can no longer afford refrigeration technology. The UN Framework

Convention on Climate Change already costs as much as the Montreal Protocol, is backed up by even less sound science, and may cost trillions of dollars if it one day manages to reduce, rather than just slow the acceleration of, carbon dioxide emissions. The Basle Convention on Transboundary Movement of Hazardous Wastes could be as costly and targets poor countries by not allowing them to trade in the waste products in which they have a comparative advantage. (Second-hand clothes are waste under the strict rules of Basle.) All these conventions can be considered destined to remain for the foreseeable future. None serves a valuable purpose.

The environmental disasters of Eastern Europe showed the folly of command and control. It is time for a new approach: environmentalists on the Right of the political spectrum must realize that the Left is using the international arena for yet more *dirigiste* experimentation – socialism works, the scale was not large enough before. The environmental Left must realize that, while they may force through international treaties, big business will still have its say and move the costs onto the poorest in society. Those environmentalists without a political ideology must realize that local solutions to local problems are no panacea but at least address the issue. International environmental treaties benefit those who draft and enact them, but no one else.

24 What some old bones in Britain can tell us

Wall Street Journal Europe (24 December 1996)

Modern societies have a healthy propensity to debunk and distrust and that has left few professionals unscathed. Lawyers the world over are the butts of jokes, accountants are increasingly accused of malpractice and doctors are more often deemed incompetent, but the reputations of academic scientists have remained high. Scientists are, on the whole, seen as admirable truth seekers, who have established and sustained their own impeccable standards of professional behaviour. Every now and then, however, a fraud is perpetrated and since they are so rare it becomes a major scandal. John Walsh's scientific detective story, *Unravelling Piltdown: The science fraud of the century and its solution* (Random House, 1996), claims to resolve the mystery of the Piltdown fraud by exposing the supposed perpetrator and how he allegedly fooled the brightest minds of Britain for forty years.

In 1911 fragments of skull were found in a gravel pit in West Sussex, England. Piecing them together revealed a half-man, half-ape creature, who revolutionized evolutionary understanding. Christened Piltdown man, it took until 1953 before the whole discovery was debunked, when Oxford University anthropologist, Joseph Wiener showed that Piltdown man was not the missing evolutionary link and had never existed. According to Walsh, 'the Piltdown fraud was nothing short of despicable, an ugly trick played by a warped and unscrupulous mind on unsuspecting scholars'. What Walsh does is retrace the steps of the crime and argues that Charles Dawson, a lawyer and amateur palaeontologist, was the perpetrator. Dawson discovered the fossils and, naturally, became a celebrity for his findings.

Walsh explains how Dawson allegedly acted, planting slivers of a 600-year-old human skull next to an ape's jawbone with two molars still attached filed down to look like human teeth. The impression given was that the separate specimens came from the same creature. Dawson contacted the Geology Department within the Natural History Museum in London, and convinced the chief curator, Arthur Smith Woodward, that the findings merited attention. Together they began digging in the gravel pit of the Sussex Estate to discover further evidence to confirm Dawson's original discovery. The bones fooled nearly everyone into thinking this was a major breakthrough, at least for a while.

Walsh eloquently describes the acrimonious disagreements at the academic meetings convened to discuss the veracity of Dawson's discoveries. Every time doubt was raised that the bones came from the same animal, a miraculously well-timed new discovery by Dawson assuaged all but the strongest critics. For over forty years evolutionary theorists were thrown into disarray because they had to take the Piltdown findings seriously, even if they were sceptical of them. Of course, once Piltdown was exposed it brought shame on their profession.

These kinds of incidents make scientists take fraud very seriously. In October, for example, faked genetic research by a scientist at the National Centre for Human Genome Research in the USA was immediately exposed once the fraud was discovered. Francis Collins, head of the centre, recalled the five papers that had been accepted for academic publication based on the false data. He apologized to colleagues in a widely circulated letter in which he explained that one researcher in his team had, unbeknownst to the rest of the team, fabricated some of the DNA sequences for one gene. In the public arena, reputations might be enhanced by the honesty and bravery shown in admitting such fraud, but public house cleaning rarely does more than polish the surfaces. The real danger is, of course, the systematic tolerance of minor fraud. Most people outside the science profession, and many inside, are not even aware of the procedural irregularities that occur.

As Alvan Feinstein, Professor of Epidemiology at Yale University, recently revealed about the elder statesmen in his profession 'I doubt . . . [they] will try to institute reforms of the defective methods that they have created, disseminated, built into the peer review process, coerced into grant approvals, and used as foundations and stepping stones for their careers and elevated status'. Unfortunately, Dr Feinstein's characterization of this kind of chronic abuse of scientific integrity is not really news, so many continue to believe that the scientific process is pure and absolutely objective.

Dramatic examples, such as Piltdown man, are useful in exposing major fraud, but they tacitly mischaracterize the problem of misinformation in research fields. Walsh actually is playing into the hands of those who like to distinguish between the purity of most science and the harm of some tiny minority who are unscrupulous. Scientists, like journalists, do not like grey areas; they like to see fraud against a background of purity, black versus white. It gives the impression of honour to scientists and drama to journalists.

But a book on the minor misrepresentations that scientists engage in would not have been as interesting as a major fraud like the Piltdown man, which Walsh exposes in his very readable book. Of course Walsh may not be right, Dawson may be innocent, someone else may have planted the evidence, but Piltdown man is discredited forever, and for this we owe Walsh a debt of thanks. His book should be read by those who still think that scientists are not like the rest of humanity. Scientists are not machine-like objective truth seekers but just human beings. Ambition, jealousy or simply impatience can tempt a scientist as well as the rest of us. Until we realize this, we will always be shocked by the Piltdown affairs of this world.

25 Cry wolf is what Greens do best

Letter to *Financial Times* (19 August 1997)

Sir, It was good to see that the FT has not lost its ability, in these politically correct times, to analyse an issue on its merits.

Your leader 'Protesters in deep water' (12 August) accurately portrayed the level of scientific uncertainty still surrounding the climate debate as well as the 'risible' campaign that Greenpeace has been mounting against the continuing exploration for oil by Shell and BP.

I have watched and assessed Greenpeace's activities over the years and have become less and less convinced by it. For example, this present campaign began in the 1970s, based on its 'limits to growth' arguments and its claims that we would soon run out of oil. However, energy prices continue to fall and the oil shortage and lower growth have still not arisen.

Ironically, the Greens insist that we now fulfil their early prophecies by abandoning oil exploration. Greenpeace demands that we must develop alternative, more expensive, and far less efficient, energy sources because burning fossil fuels induces global warming.

But is man-made warming likely to be dangerous? Anyone who is old enough to remember the 'imminent ice age' scare of twenty-five years ago will know that crying wolf is what Greens do best.

Despite the fact that the world is getting safer and cleaner as wealth increases, Greenpeace may still find an issue worthy of its attention. However, like the little boy who cried wolf, it may have lost the interest of a responsible public irritated by its continued alarmist rants.

26 How the media short-change business

Wall Street Journal Europe (14 August 1997)

One of the greatest dangers to democracy, which depends on healthy public discourse, is the deliberate exclusion of certain voices from the debate. Unfortunately, that practice is increasingly common among journalists eager to sensationalize science and health issues in search of catchy headlines.

Consider the sound and fury over toxic shock syndrome (TSS). Last week British Prime Minister Tony Blair announced that new women's focus groups would make sure that his government was in touch with the female perspective on key policy issues. One of the issues that pressure groups are urging them to consider is why big business is endangering female voters with sanitary hygiene products.

Although it might please these focus groups to expose the TSS health scare cover up by big business, the scare is nothing more than cheap journalism manipulating women's fears.

TSS is an extremely rare condition caused by a toxin produced by the bacterium *Staphylococcus aureus*, which can afflict anyone following injury or surgery. Although not new, it was first described in 1978 in America and became famous in 1980 when a rash of fatalities in menstruating women led epidemiologists to track down a potential cause – new, high-absorbency tampons. The sponge-like product linked to the scare, sold only in America, was removed and the number of deaths in all categories of TSS patients fell to less than a dozen annually.

Nevertheless, any fatality is worthy of continuing investigation, and a conference in a few weeks at the Royal Society of Medicine in London will see the world's leading TSS experts present their latest findings. This conference is backed by the tampon manufacturers who want to know if their products are a risk factor for TSS. Even if tampons are a risk factor, given that there are some 14 million menstruating women in the UK, using over a billion tampons annually, the odds on contracting a fatal case of TSS from using tampons are tiny, and far lower than being struck by lightening.

Yet last summer the *Mail on Sunday* ran an article with the headline 'Hundreds of women are dying of an unspoken illness', which alarmingly claimed that one in four women could be affected by TSS. A week later a TV advertisement was aired which featured a tampon with a burning fuse, much like a time bomb. This vivid imagery was endorsed by a wide variety of pressure groups, such as the Women's Environmental Network. Manufacturers protested about the gross factual inaccuracies in the article and advertisement, but all their remarks went unheeded. Litigation was their only option, which they declined.

While the media have lately become very sophisticated at gathering information from myriad international sources, businesses are rarely given a fair hearing. It is easy for a journalist or environmental expert to dismiss an industry spokesman with explicit or implied comments such as, 'well, he would say that, wouldn't he?'.

Another discouraging incident happened in May, when Heinz Rothermund, Managing Director of Shell Exploration and Production, gave a speech at the University of Strathclyde about the essential role of energy in the world economy. He spoke of the environmental and cost dilemmas that may in the future curtail some of Shell's explorations west of the Shetland Islands. Immediately following this, Greenpeace Campaigns Director Chris Rose issued a wildly distorted press statement announcing Rothermund's supposed admission that 'there is no scientific, political or moral justification for continued oil exploration'. Rose continued 'this is an extraordinary admission which must lead to a change in government and oil industry policy'. The Shell press office strenuously denied that Rothermund had said anything of the sort but declined to ask Greenpeace for a retraction as, according to a spokesman, they did not want to 'escalate' the issue. Continuing its campaign last month, Greenpeace demanded an immediate halt to oil exploration around the globe, and Shell officials, in an amazing display of accommodation, went to meet with them.

Because the Shell executives, probably like other company directors affected by health, safety and environment issues, feel that they can only lose from a confrontation with a pressure group or the media, they back down and appease. What is so sad is that, from a strategic point of view, they are probably right to do so. After all, during the *Brent Spar* farce, activists firebombed Shell petrol stations and attacked directors' homes.

Attacking big business may seem to be a victimless indulgence, but this should be of great concern to consumers because false product or service information, disseminated by third-party groups, may go unchallenged by business because of justifiable fears by company directors that they will not be believed.

Perhaps worse is that *ad hominem* attacks on business are bread and butter to certain television producers desperate to find sensational stories. Last summer I was approached by a consultant to the new BBC series, *Sci Files*. As a global-warming sceptic who has been on several TV and radio shows, I was not surprised to be asked to attend a preliminary interview at the BBC to discuss the format of the show. They seemed very interested in my sources of funding, and I was not asked back for filming. Although I can't be sure why, it's interesting that the three American academics they eventually interviewed held views similar to mine, yet unlike me, received support from fossil-fuel industries. The programme used implications of bias to rubbish their reputations, omitted their university accreditations, reported things out of context, and made them look shifty or cavalier. *Sci Files* played on the fact that business funded research is unusual in Europe, where only the findings of publicly financed university research is completely trusted.

It is unfortunate that industry scientists, who may be world experts on an issue like hygiene products, cannot take a fair part in scientific debate. After all, consumers have to pay in terms of lesser products and higher prices as companies withdraw safe lines that have been denounced by lobbyists. For example, the TSS scare has been hijacked by some environmentalists who claim that synthetic pesticides and chemicals in tampons are partly responsible for TSS. There is absolutely no evidence for this, but companies have been falling over themselves to introduce cotton-only tampons.

Tampons, once the symbol of freedom for women, have become stigmatized as a health hazard. A Taylor Nelson business consultancy survey shows that in the past five years there has been a 17 per cent reduction of tampon use in the UK, with a switch to other hygiene products, notably pads. Ironically, the company most closely associated with the first TSS scare, Procter & Gamble Co., whose tampon 'Rely' had to be withdrawn in the early 1980s, has just bought Tambrands Ltd, the producers of market leader Tampax. P&G must be praying that they have better luck in the tampon market than they did fifteen years ago. Unfortunately, in today's climate of fear, engendered by health and environmental scaremongers, their success is not in their hands, but on media pressure on an increasingly jittery female customer. Let's hope that Blair's wise women see through the manipulation and let businesses have their say.

27 Stop the madness

The Wall Street Journal Europe (23 December 1997)

Just when you thought it was safe to eat beef again, another scare comes along to reinvigorate the mad cow crisis. Last Tuesday the Blair government announced that it will snatch British boned beef (T-bone steaks, oxtails and ribs) off holiday plates for fear that it carries the dreaded mad cow disease (BSE) inside the bone marrow.

To further aggravate the situation, concern about the safety of beef is leading to an escalation of agricultural protectionism within the European Union and the United States. The crisis is spiralling out of control once again, even though the risk posed by British meat is ridiculously minuscule, a fact which has British farmers and consumers asking whether it is the officials and not the cows who have gone mad.

The start of the crisis came twenty-one months ago when the EU banned British beef because of fears that cows fed with animal parts could develop BSE, which some scientists contend causes the degenerative and fatal new-variant Creutzfeldt-Jakob disease (CJD) in humans. In an effort to deal with the threat, the UK Agricultural Ministry ordered millions of cattle slaughtered costing British taxpayers $10 billion. Under pressure from the EU, the Ministry also pushed through new legislation, which ensures that all spinal cords and brains of cattle, sheep and goats are not used for animal feed.

Despite the fact that British beef is now subject to more stringent tests than cattle from other EU countries, the ban on Britain's beef remains. This understandably annoyed British farmers. In response, UK Agricultural Minister Jack Cunningham announced that he will ban beef imports to Britain from countries that do not live up to the new British standards. 'If our European colleagues don't take the action that I believe is necessary . . . their meat will not come into Britain', he warned at an EU agriculture ministers' meeting last week. The ban starts on 1 January, but to show his European partners that he will also not tolerate *any* risk from British beef, even if eaten domestically, Mr Cunningham banned British boned beef.

At the same time the USA announced that it will ban most beef and lamb from all fifteen EU countries (including the six with no BSE cases) because of fears over mad cow disease. Last week, the EU announced that a reciprocal ban will begin in six months unless the USA increases checks on unnatural levels in American meat products of hormones and antibiotics widely regarded by scientists as being safe. The ban would cover American beef derivatives such as gelatine, which would include $4 billion worth of American pharmaceuticals.

What's been lost in all the bans and counter-bans are the facts. Some 170,000 BSE cases have been found among British cattle, apparently because of the practice of feeding cows, which are herbivores, with the remains of other animals. However, about twenty cases of nvCJD have surfaced – there's a possibility more may occur as we do not know the incubation period of the disease, but the chances are remote given the time passed already. One of the many sceptical scientists, Gordon Stewart, Emeritus Professor of Public Health at Glasgow University, asserts that the link between BSE and nvCJD is still not properly established, and whatever risk there was has now likely passed because the cause of BSE has been taken out of the food chain.

However, even if one accepts the science behind the latest UK ban on boned beef, the risk to the public is acknowledged as being so tiny as to be meaningless. Dr Cunningham's move followed advice from the British government's Spongiform Encephalopathy Advisory Committee (SEAC) that there was a theoretical risk that cattle bone marrow could transmit BSE. SEAC explained that unless the government took action there was a 5 per cent chance that one person in the UK would contract CJD from beef on the bone in 1998.

Thus, no bones are to be sold for soup or even the family dog, even though the odds of contracting this form of CJD are roughly one in one billion. In other words, a Briton is about 100 times more likely to be struck by lightening, 4000 times more likely to choke to death, 10,000 times more likely to be murdered, 40,000 times more likely to die on a football field or from ingesting carcinogens from eating potatoes or parsnips and 100,000 times more likely to die in a road accident than contract CJD from a rib of beef.

Fortunately the average Briton knows that beef is safe, which is why after Dr Cunningham's latest ban they did not strike beef from the menu, but descended in droves upon butchers to buy up the last ribs and steaks in time for Christmas. My own butcher would not sell me a T-bone steak this week, not because he was concerned about becoming an outlaw, but because he had run out.

According to repeated news reports, butchers all over Britain are flouting the new law. *The Daily Telegraph* reported that Paul Robinson, a butcher from Andover in Hampshire, is prepared to risk the six months in jail and a $3300 fine to sell boned beef. Ludicrously, anyone will still be able to buy beef on the bone from wholesalers, simply by claiming to be in a catering company, or representing a pub or restaurant. These food 'experts' are deemed by Blair's nanny government as capable of safely de-boning and cooking meat, whereas the rest of the population is not.

Given that the new law is not necessary to protect public health and that it is being widely ignored, the next question is why the Agriculture Department announced the ban at all. One possible explanation is that Jack Cunningham is trying to show other EU farm ministers that he means business. In other words, he may have taken the extreme measure of prohibiting boned beef, as well as proposing a ban on EU beef, simply to encourage the lifting of the ban on British beef. There is, as yet, little evidence to confirm this, but when British farmers were caught recently throwing imported meat into the sea at Holyhead port near Liverpool, Jack Cunningham's reprimand was slow in coming.

It is too early to say whether the crisis is heading for resolution or escalation, but the latter could have serious economic ramifications. A USA–EU beef war could significantly undermine the liberalizations won – especially with regard to agriculture – during the last GATT round. This would be a disaster for the world's consumers. It would also affect developing countries (and Eastern Europe) as their economies are dominated by agricultural products that may be hindered by Western trade barriers. Now is the time for cooler heads to prevail, lest the madness spread.

28 Hysteria – a media-caused disease

Unpublished

According to many media reports, our concerns about our health and safety range from man-made pollutants to satanic ritual abuse, especially where these manifestations threaten other people, less resilient or less aware than ourselves. Professor Elaine Showalter of Princeton University has analysed modern attitudes to risk and explains why they have changed and what the media's role might be. Trained in literary criticism, she has earned a significant reputation as a leading feminist historian of psychiatry.

Given the hostility that has surrounded her latest book *Hystories: Hysterical Epidemics and Modern Media* (Picador, 1997), it is as well that she has such an esteemed reputation. Other than threats, she has endured physical assault for her provocative thesis: modern forms of hysteria, including sexual addiction problems, Gulf War Syndrome, multiple personality disorder, satanic ritual abuse, and alien abduction, are primarily psychological disorders rather than physiological conditions. According to Showalter, some patients believe psychosomatic disorders are socially unacceptable. Therefore, in their very real 'hysterical' distress, they 'search for physical evidence that firmly places cause and cure outside the self', thereby expressing their pain and conflict in the form of the culturally-acceptable language of body illness.

What makes Showalter's thesis so controversial is that she claims that popular Hollywood productions featuring alien abduction and scary science fiction have contributed to the malaise. It's not just feature films, but all media including newspapers, magazines, the internet, self-help books and talk shows, that spread the culturally fashionable narratives she terms 'hystories'. She explains how patients learn about diseases from the media and unconsciously develop symptoms – a common phenomenon among trainee doctors, including psychiatrists. The familiar 'plot lines' in our culture (e.g. what an 'X-files' alien looks like or how satanic abuse is conducted) explain how hysterical patients can independently tell the same story. In essence, she is claiming that hysteria is a communicable disease and the media are the primary vector.

The most interesting part of her analysis is that she believes that the media can be an effective point of intervention. If the media are the cause, so they can be the cure. Showalter claims that we can 'use the media to fight rumours as well as to spread them'. She is even rather optimistic about the possibility of combating the 'X-filing' of America giving several examples of where serious scientists, such as UFO investigators, have distanced themselves from discussions of alien abduction. In UK, Michael White's book *Science of the X-files* (Legend Books, 1996) has done much to show the difference between science fact and science fiction. Furthermore, journalists such as Robert Matthews, Nigel Hawkes and Steve Connor regularly put the record straight. According to Showalter, other fightbacks are springing up from such disparate sources as women's lobbies and conservative pro-science groups like The Advancement of Sound Science Coalition.

One only has to look at the current 'inflation' of alleged addictions to see the dangers of scientifically literate people failing to point out the absurdity of some claims. Addiction used to have a strong physiological meaning: a substance or activity was craved in increasing doses and there had to be an element of intoxication for addiction to be diagnosed. Heroin was addictive, nicotine was not; it was considered to be a habit, hard to kick, but a habit none the less. But while it is commonplace to incorrectly misdiagnose nicotine as addictive in its proper sense, we now have internet addiction, chocoholics anonymous, and the pathology of scratch cards. Applying the medical label of addiction to bad habits, devalues the term and celebrates irresponsibility and victimhood.

As Frank Furedi's book *Culture of Fear* (Cassell, 1997) has shown, our self-conscious victim-inspired culture has inadvertently spawned an infectious form of blame hysteria, where the individual is the last person to accept responsibility for their actions – abuse at childhood or industrial chemicals are favourite targets for blame. Professor Showalter adds a new dimension however, she explains that in an effort to lend further credence to these ailments, even earning an official diagnosis from the medical establishment – making health insurance easier to obtain – we are probably worsening the health problems of psychosomatic patients. Allowing patients to persistently cry wolf – such as over satanic child abuse – inevitably leads doctors to believe that there is no wolf. For some patients this will be the case, but wolves do exist, and those patients who have encountered them will probably not be believed.

Anyone who aims to improve scientific literacy will thoroughly enjoy and approve of Professor's Showalter's attempt (and success) at improving psychological literacy. Understanding (be it of science or psychology) is not a sufficient condition for acceptance of reality but it is a necessary one.

29 Statistical snake-oil

Unpublished

Why is it that many medical breakthroughs, which seem so promising when first reported, seem to vanish without a trace? Also why is it that every week we hear of a new deadly food or other health scare, yet we are living longer than ever?

Over the years, many more or less plausible explanations have evolved. Some have blamed over-reliance on results from small samples. Others have focused on so-called 'publication bias', the reluctance of researchers to submit – and academic journals to print – negative findings from early studies (see Bate ed., *What Risk?* Butterworth-Heinemann, 1997, viii–ix, for my earlier discussion). The fact that patients in medical trials tend to be fussed over and given the best possible care by dedicated experts may also play some role.

But there is another explanation – one with profound implications for all scientific research. Its existence has been known within academic circles for years, and leading experts have repeatedly warned of its potentially dire consequences for the reliability of scientific research. Yet to this day, no decisive action has ever been taken to deal with it.

A clue to its identity comes from the one feature all of these scientific disciplines have in common: they all rely on so-called 'significance tests' to gauge the importance of their findings. Introduced during the early part of this century, these statistical tests are routinely used throughout the scientific community. Thousands of scientific papers and millions of pounds of research funding have been based on their conclusions. They are ubiquitous and easy to use. And they are fundamentally and dangerously flawed.

Science writer and physicist, Robert Matthews, has exposed this flaw in a recent publication called *Statistical Snake-Oil* (Feb. 1999) written for ESEF (see www.esef.org). Used to analyse clinical trials, he has explained that these textbook techniques can easily double the apparent effectiveness of a new drug or treatment, and turn a borderline result into a highly 'significant' breakthrough. They can throw up convincing, yet utterly spurious, evidence for 'links' between diseases and any number of supposed causes. The result is an ever-growing amount of research across the whole scientific spectrum whose conclusions are based on techniques known for decades to be unreliable. And all because scientists want to avoid being accused of subjectivity.

Matthews explains that 'subjectivity is seen as the barbarian at the gates of science, the enemy of objective truth'. So when the Cambridge mathematician Ronald Fisher came up with an apparently objective way of drawing conclusions from experiments in the 1920s, it was adopted almost overnight.

Central to Fisher's analysis is the *P*-value, which is defined as the chances of getting at least as impressive evidence by luck. Fisher arbitrarily selected a cut-off point of 0.05, so that a result is considered significant if it is below 0.05. The impact of this cut-off level is stark. Open any scientific journal and you will see the phrase, '$P < 0.05$', and it is used in drug approval in this country and many others.

But Matthews has shown that no sooner was the Fisher 'test' being used than questions began to be asked about why $P > 0.05$ was considered 'significant'. After all, if it is used to approve a new drug it should stand up to criticism. Apparently, Fisher just claimed it was 'convenient'. There is no good reason. It was subjectively chosen.

The other related problem with the Fisher cut-off is that it is not enough of a test in today's nervous commercial world. A product stands to be banned (following a scare) or approved (following medical testing) by a set of results which may be inconclusive. Mathematicians in the 1950s and 1960s showed that the Fisher cut-off of 5 per cent ($P < 0.05$) can lead to flukes far more than 5 per cent of the time. On the face of it, Fisher's P-value standard of 0.05 means that the chances of mere fluke being the real explanation for a given result is just 5 in 100 – plenty of protection against being fooled. But this is not what P-values mean. What they actually give is the probability of seeing results at least as impressive as those obtained, *assuming* that mere chance is their true explanation.

This oddly convoluted definition of a P-value is the first symptom of all that is wrong with standard significance testing. For it shows that the P-value is the answer to a question researchers are rarely interested in. Why should anyone give a hoot about 'at least as impressive' results that would have appeared *assuming* fluke were their cause? What researchers are really interested in is something far simpler – the chances that the effect really is just a fluke, given the data actually obtained.

Yet this is a question P-values cannot answer – and thinking that they can is a blunder routinely made by many working scientists and even statistics textbooks. The result is that papers are published showing a significant result, which may be, and often is, bogus.

Fisher's approach replaced the more overtly subjective Bayes' theorem, which had been used since the late eighteenth century. It was named after its inventor Thomas Bayes, the cleric and mathematician. Bayes' theorem was a recipe to update one's belief in a theory as new evidence emerged. But before one can use Bayes' theorem one has to have a belief in the plausibility of success of the experiment underway. In short, the more sceptical one is, the more information one needs to be convinced that the experiment is valid. And of course, this is subjective. But as more data emerge, the opinions of a rational 'sceptic' and a rational 'believer' will converge. Bayes' approach drives one to constant re-evaluation of the subject matter.

Bayes' theorem provides the only way to find out the answer to the questions that scientists really want from P-values – the chances that mere fluke *really is* the explanation of data.

As a result of the problems with Fisher's approach, the editor of the respected *American Journal of Public Health*, Professor Kenneth Rothman, decided in 1986 to no longer accept papers with just P-values. Two years after he retired the journal reverted to P-values. The main reason according to Matthews is because of inertia in the academic profession to change. All the student textbooks, teachers and funding rely on P-values, and so they remain. 'If scientists abandon significance tests like P-values, many of their claims would be seen for what they really are: meaningless aberrations on which taxpayers' money should never have been spent', claims Matthews.

30 Press release non-science

Economic Affairs (June 1999)

What do toxic toys, the Arctic ozone hole and passive smoking-induced lung cancer have in common? All of them were announced in speculative press releases, which claimed that subsequent research in peer reviewed journals would demonstrate the veracity of the original claims. Yet we are still awaiting the research, the allegations remain unsubstantiated.

If these claims were made within the scientific community to simply encourage debate then there would be no problem, but in all these cases, pressure group press releases resulted in media coverage. Inevitably policy has been enacted to deal with the putative problem, often under focus group pressure induced by hysterical media coverage.

Perhaps the worst of the three examples is the first. Polyvinylchloride (PVC) is a ubiquitous and versatile material, its uses ranging from blood bags and other medical uses to guttering. It has also been used in children's toys for decades. PVC is rigid and to make it more malleable, softeners called phthalates are added to it. Environmental groups claim that these phthalates migrate from the plastic in toys to the mouth when chewed by young children. They further claim that phthalates are carcinogenic, may reduce sperm counts, and have other hormone effects.

These groups put pressure on manufacturers such as Mattel and Toys Я Us to withdraw products that used phthalates claiming they killed children. They also demanded a worldwide ban of the products. In response, the EU initiated studies into the migration of phthalates from chewed toys and the dangers they may pose. As I write these studies are ongoing, but are rapidly becoming irrelevant, as country after country threatens to ban phthalates saying they must act with precaution if there is a threat to children's health.

According to Bill Durodié, of the Health Unit of the London School of Economics, and author of *Poisonous Dummies* (July 1999) (see www.esef.org), which documents the PVC saga, the influence of the BSE debacle is making matters worse. The European Parliament must now take minority scientific views into account when analysing any scare. This means that activist allegations, which contradict all major scientific studies, carry the same weight in deliberations as scientific studies. In fact they carry more weight if, as is the case with phthalate toxicity, the European Parliament bases its safety levels on worst-case scenarios. It is likely that the EU scientific studies will report no danger at ambient levels from phthalates, but employing worst-case scenarios and unscientifically large safety factors, the EU will surely recommend a ban.

But even precautionary bans may not be necessary as companies, loath to see negative headlines about their products, voluntarily withdraw phthalate-plasticized toys.

Now that the EU has taken up the activists' part on toys, the slick campaigners have moved onto their next target – medical products. Surely if toys are harmful, then blood bags and medical tubing must be as well. Indeed, Stockholm County Council (SCC) has decided to phase out the use of PVC medical products.

Baxter Healthcare Ltd, producers of medical PVC products, has so far maintained the commitment to PVC. Baxter's Environmental Manager, Birgitta Lindblom, said that the SCC decision 'may have tragic consequences for many people'. Nevertheless Baxter may have to find alternatives following the SCC decision. But according to Bill Durodié the alternatives are less well known and may pose a greater relative risk. Will they too be banned on the altar of precaution?

Phthalate-softened PVC has been used for decades, and as Durodié says 'there is not a single shred of evidence that it has ever harmed any human being'. The scientific research time involved in analysing phthalate toxicity is detracting from work that could be done into real, rather than virtual, risks. However, the greatest harm of pressure group-inspired scares, such as on PVC, is the distrust of scientific research it encourages. When a press release from Greenpeace can carry the same weight (or more given worse-case scenarios) than a peer reviewed scientific study, it's really time to worry.

But it gets worse still. Governments and intergovernmental agencies are adopting the Greens' tactics to push through their favourite policies. In the past three years we have seen various UN climate and ozone treaty documents altered by officials (so they agreed with previous summaries and press releases) to further the role of energy taxes, and ban a widely-used pesticide.

Press release science is the retreat from reason, and until it is arrested, we will see numerous products go the way of PVC toys.

31 Unsafe at any price? Different standards for organic luvvies

Wall Street Journal Europe (15 November 1999)

Imagine you saw a TV programme called *The Open Road* – a magazine show about cars sponsored by Ford and supported by a newspaper campaign. You'd most likely view it as little more than an infomercial and treat it with the appropriate amount of scepticism. Now imagine you saw a show about the joys of growing and cooking your own organic fruits and vegetables, sponsored by a commercial organic producer and with the backing of a trendy, left-wing paper. Wouldn't you be as sceptical? Well apparently not if you're British.

Channel Four television, in league with *The Guardian* newspaper, have just stepped over the boundary of commercial fairness by allowing direct promotion of such a show, without raising a peep of protest from the British public.

Last weekend saw the beginning of *Fork to Fork*, a new four-part Channel Four series that demonstrates the wonders of organic farming to British households. The beautiful organic garden owned by presenter Monty Don is lovingly cared for 'without the use of chemicals', he explains. Of course, he means without the use of *synthetic* chemicals, but this misrepresentation really sets the tone of the programme. It's fun, slightly condescending, and reinforces the unscientific myths of organic farming.

Monty Don's almost pornographic enjoyment of just-uprooted fast-cooked new potatoes, and his interesting advice about controlling pests with wooden fencing, fleece and chives, was mildly enjoyable. Less so were the commercial breaks. The jarring voice-overs from the sponsor of the programme announced 'Seeds of Change: 100 per cent organic foods', sprang to the viewers' attention. I thought back to the show's romantic images of the country garden and the oak-beamed kitchen, selling the rural idyll to urbanites, and felt conned. Did no one else see the connection?

Seeds of Change, a supreme irony, is an American company based in Santa Fe, New Mexico. Established in 1989, their web site proudly claims that they 'are concerned about conventional farming methods which . . . rely upon pesticides, herbicides and chemical fertilizers'. Instead of intensive farming they are committed to an organic way of life, producing crops without resorting to artificial pesticides, fertilizers, hormones or antibiotics and not using advanced genetic techniques. In short, farming without most of the scientific advances made in the past seventy years. They are intent on selling these ideas and their company name into other countries. As such they benefit, like any business, in promoting their product, and subtly undermining the opposition.

They and their organic brothers have been decidedly successful. The UK market for organic food has grown from £40 million ten years ago to £1 billion in 1998. The massive expansion in provision has attracted big business. Wholesome big business no doubt, but big business.

Seeds of Change has been advertising in the past few weeks, probably to coincide with the launch of *Fork to Fork*. They are being very creative; bus stops are adorned with their posters in the trendy London Borough of Islington, where Prime Minister Tony Blair used to live. They know that the market for their produce is middle-class urbanites who want to feel they can get back in touch with nature by consuming organic produce. Furthermore, last month they sponsored an eight-page pull-out section of *The Guardian*, called 'Easy steps to organic living'. In one article there is even advice on how to raise an organic baby.

The polling agency MORI recently asked British people various questions about organic food. The results show that over half those who buy it think that organic food is 'healthier'. But is organic food really so wholesome? And should a baby be eating organic produce?

A baby has an immature immune system and is more easily infected with germs than adults. Yet in the whole web site of Seeds of Change, or *Fork to Fork*, there is no mention of the dangers of home-grown organic produce, which may contain more toxins and bacteria than normal foods. After all, these nasties are not being destroyed by synthetic pesticides, since organic farmers won't use them, whereas compost and manure, the foundation of organic farm nutrients, are breeding grounds for bacteria and fungi.

According to Dennis Avery, of the Hudson Institute in Niagara, there is a greater chance of contracting the potentially fatal *E. coli* from eating organic food than normal food. And according to Anthony Trewavas, Professor of Cell Biology at Edinburgh University, a whole host of bacterial infections, including salmonella, are more likely to be caught from eating organic food. Furthermore, according to Professor Bruce Ames of UC Berkeley, one of the world's leading biochemists, there is no evidence of any health benefits from eating organic produce. You are no more likely to get cancer from eating an insecticide-sprayed apple than from eating an organic apple because the level of natural pesticides produced by the apple dwarfs those of man-made spraying. And if you eat fewer organic apples, because they are more expensive, you will in fact be worse off as fruit contains chemicals which guard against cancer. Yet *The Guardian* and the equally 'hip' Channel Four raise none of these arguments. They are happy to be co-opted by a commercial enterprise to help them lure Brits into buying their organic products and expand their market.

And there's nothing wrong with a company wanting to increase market share. Only that the directors of Monsanto and other American agro-chemical companies must be crying in their sleep, if they can get any sleep at the moment. While their new technologies are attacked by every conceivable pressure group and most newspapers, they have to sit and watch more dangerous rival products being promoted on TV. With such obvious double standards operating at a prestigious television network and a liberal newspaper, is it any wonder that the public are moving in droves towards organic food. But poor parents care about their families just like middle-class ones, yet if organic food becomes the middle-class norm, the poor will probably feel they must join in, convinced that otherwise they will be harming their children.

The owners of Seeds of Change must be laughing all the way to their, no doubt, ecological bank. Perhaps in this politically correct environment it isn't even remarkable that consumers are prepared to pay more for food that is more dangerous. But organic food really is less safe – whatever the price.

Part Three

Regulation and Rent-seeking

32 What am I bid?

Economic Affairs (September–October 1993)

How does one value the delight one feels at the mere existence of the New Forest or Snowdonia? 'Easy!' cry many environmental economists 'ask a stratified sample of British people how much they are willing to pay to preserve the site and use the mean figure multiplied by the population of Britain as the existence value of each site. Right?' In an attempt to overcome the information problem, which is seen within mainstream economics as one of the causes of market failure (and the reason given for much government intervention), many environmental economists have developed a survey technique to produce such existence values from 'willingness to pay' (WTP) responses. This technique is called contingent valuation (CV): the valuation of an amenity, such as Snowdonia, is contingent upon the hypothetical market that the surveyors envisage might exist.

Environmental economists recognize that responses to questionnaires are sometimes an incorrect indication of the actual behaviour of the respondents. They have, therefore, systematically analysed the measurement problems associated with these techniques. I shall highlight two of these problems.

First, anyone who has seen the TV game show *The Price is Right* will have noticed that the contestants' knowledge of consumer goods prices varies enormously. In general, the contestants will know, within a few pounds, the prices of those goods they normally purchase. However (and this is the strength of the programme and a weakness of contingent valuation) when they are asked the price of something they do not normally buy (such as lacquered fountain-pens) they will not have the vaguest clue as to their value.

Similarly, individuals are, not surprisingly, insufficiently informed to assess the monetary value of environmental amenities. In many cases, they will never have heard of the resource and consequently a CV survey may create the value it is purporting to measure.

Second, as the respondents will not be asked to hand over the amount they say they are willing to pay, the figure they state may be vastly higher than they would actually pay. For example, an environmentalist who believes that the government does not spend enough on wildlife protection could state their WTP as being most of their income, giving an answer orders of magnitude higher than they would contribute.

There are many other statistical problems with CV data, too numerous to discuss in this article. However, there is one crucial methodological reason, largely overlooked by environmental economists, for never using CV surveys for valuation purposes. There is a fundamental difference between people's behaviour, as observed in the market (choice or revealed preference), and the answers they may give to hypothetical questions about their behaviour (stated preference). Willingness to pay figures are assumed, by proponents of contingent valuation studies, to be synonymous with choice. These economists draw no distinction between choice (revealed preference) and WTP (stated preference).

However, WTP constitutes, at most, a disposition to choose. Choice, on the other hand, requires action – it is the behaviour itself. Choice is a superior criterion because, unlike stating one's WTP, there is a cost in being wrong and therefore there is an incentive to be accurate. If individuals, or conservation groups, wish to preserve a natural resource they can purchase it. Their action expresses consent, engagement and commitment. In making a choice they become accountable and responsible for it. Stating a WTP may mean they can preserve the resource without incurring any cost to themselves.

Therefore, however statistically reliable such CV survey results may be, the fundamental flaw of using stated preferences rather than revealed preferences will always exist when using surveys for valuation.

I am sure by now you are asking: 'OK, so surveys are flawed. So what? What's the point to all this?'

Consider how the United States Department of Commerce (DOC) is using CV surveys. DOC is promulgating regulations, endorsing CV survey use, for assessing liability for injuries to the 'existence value' of natural resources caused by discharges of hazardous substances and petroleum. Existence values calculated by 'CV studies can produce estimates reliable enough to be the starting point for a judicial . . . determination of natural resource damages' (DOC advisers' judgement on CV use 13 January 1993). Exxon had to spend over $6 million on CV surveys after the *Valdez* oil spill in Alaska.

The European Commission's 'Green Paper on Remedying Environmental Damage' (Com (93) 47) contemplates a similar overall liability structure to that in the USA, at present without the measurement of existence values. It may not be that long before they are on the agenda this side of the Atlantic as well. You have been warned.

33 Cambridge Water: What was missed

Economic Affairs (April 1994)

The recent Cambridge Water case is considered one of the most important common law cases of the last few decades. The House of Lords judgement was expected to define the role of common law in the protection of environmental resources. In the event, the judgement seemed to go against environmental protection. Is that true?

Prior to 1976, Eastern Counties Leather plc (ECL), a tannery operating for over a century, allowed the volatile solvent perchloroethene (PCE) to escape in small quantities from its site and leach into the groundwater. The 'contaminated' water seeped into the chalk aquifer and travelled 1.3 miles to the site of the Sawston Mill borehole, owned by the Cambridge Water Company (CWC). In 1979 CWC started to pump water for public use from the borehole. The quality met existing standards and was 'wholesome'. But in 1980 an EC Directive imposed higher water quality standards and tests carried out in 1983 at Sawston Mill showed that the water was then contaminated by PCE and considered not fit for human consumption. CWC was forced to drill another borehole costing over £1 million. In 1985 CWC sued ECL for damages equal to the cost of drilling the new borehole.

The lower court found for the defendants, holding that ECL could not have foreseen such a loss. The Court of Appeal then held that foreseeability was not a prerequisite for strict liability in nuisance. However, ECL's appeal to the House of Lords was successful as the Lords held that foreseeability was required for a claim in nuisance. The decision was greeted with headlines like 'Firms given pollution amnesty', 'Polluters let off hook by ruling' and 'Water polluter will not foot the bill'. Environmentalists argued that common law could not protect the environment and that further regulation was required.

Two important points were raised by the Lords. First, they acknowledged that there was no physical harm. 'The water so contaminated at Sawston Mill has never been held to be dangerous to health'. Second, they stated that 'it is more appropriate for strict liability to be imposed by Parliament, than by the courts. [G]iven that so much well-informed and carefully structured legislation is now being put in place for this purpose, there is little need for the courts to develop a common law principle to achieve the same end, and indeed it may be undesirable that they should do so'.

What the Lords and other commentators failed to mention was that common law requires a 'damager' to recompense the 'damaged'. The European Community Directive demands punitive retribution where there was no damage – the concentration of the chemicals was too low. What has to be considered is the *dose* of the chemicals. As has been known for centuries, the right dose differentiates a poison from a remedy.

PCE is harmful, but only at high concentrations. It is the *dose* that counts, not the presence of the chemical. Relatively new techniques, such as gas chromatography, allow small concentrations of trace compounds to be measured – down to less than one part per billion (ppb). However, just because they can be measured is no reason to regulate their use. There is a danger that regulators will take advantage of improvements in measurement technology to keep on tightening regulations.

Possibly the most over-regulated group of chemicals is pesticides. Cost-driven improvements in technology mean that whereas fifty years ago, 2 tonnes of sodium-based pesticides were used per hectare, nowadays only 10 grammes of sulphonyl-based pesticides are required. Food quality is improving and the quantities of pesticides used are falling. The EC's Drinking Water Directive allows ambient concentrations of pesticides of only 0.1 ppb, which seems excessively cautious and has no scientific basis. As John Finney of Zeneca Agrochemicals explains: 'Drinking 13.5 gallons of water is equivalent to eating one apple, as far as pesticide levels are concerned. Implementing this directive may mean that 60 per cent of pesticides will be scrapped'.

The idea that the common law cannot protect against pollution is false. The common law cannot protect against arbitrary standards imposed by government, but it does provide a remedy against harm to the environment. Common law is undermined by regulation, not enhanced by it. Deregulation of water quality standards is a prerequisite for an unencumbered, fully functioning common law system, which would genuinely protect water quality. The *dose* of the chemical, not merely its presence, must be the basis for defining 'harm'.

34 Catastrophe insurers warm to the debate

Wall Street Journal Europe (8–9 September 1995)

As the summer of 1995 goes on record as one of Europe's driest and hottest, speculation that we are finally witnessing global warming is rife. One would expect this from publicity hungry environmental groups, and perhaps even from the scientists whose research hinges on continued governmental funding. But they are not really pushing the issue at the moment as avidly as another group – the insurance industry.

Richard Keeling, lead underwriter at the Harvey Bowring Lloyds syndicate said at the Intergovernmental Conference on Climate Change held in Berlin this April, 'insurers fear that global warming is accelerating the trend towards costlier natural catastrophes'. According to another leading insurance researcher 'the speed of global warming is a problem', and is causing 'the growing number and intensity of storms'. In fact, many insurers say that some coverage may have to be withdrawn from certain locations because of the threat of climate change.

No, this most calculating of industries hasn't undergone a sudden environmental conversion. More likely, they've decided that concern about climate change might be good for the bottom line.

Some of the world's largest reinsurers, who gathered in Monte Carlo on Monday for their annual meeting, are also worried. They have said that private industry cannot be expected to cover losses caused by natural forces if they regularly affect the same region. The clincher is that some insurers have called for a greater 'risk partnership' between policy holders, insurers, reinsurers and governments. In effect the insurers want governments to be the lender of last resort in as Keeling put it, 'Armageddon scenarios'.

But is there something more than just one exceptionally warm summer fuelling this concern? The warming predictions of some primitive computer models have yet to be borne out by the data. The planet may have warmed by 0.5° Celsius since the industrial revolution, but most of this increase occurred before 1940, while most of the greenhouse gases were emitted after that. And satellite temperature measurements, which aren't biased by the urban heat-island effect that plagues land-based measurement systems, have shown no increase in global temperature in recent years. In fact, global temperature historically correlates much better with levels of solar radiation – which presumably aren't affected by anything human beings do – than with levels of carbon dioxide in the atmosphere.

The insurance business, like all financial services, was a major money-spinner of the 1980s boom, encouraging too many imprudent firms to enter the market. Less care was given to assessment of insurance risk in the scramble for business. Couple this with a string of natural disasters – winter floods, hurricanes and summer droughts – and the losses can be significant. Blaming these disasters on climate change, some are undoubtedly hoping that the taxpayers will eventually be asked to pick up the tab. According to leading reinsurer Munich Re, the insured cost of natural disasters is some fourteen times greater now than in the 1960s. But this isn't because climate change is making the world a much more dangerous place. First, the value of property has increased many times. Second, much of the world's most valuable property is located in precarious regions – no doubt encouraged by existing government forays into the disaster insurance market. Japan and California have high value property and high earthquake risks. Finally, more property is insured today than ever before as a consequence of greater wealth and the desire to protect that wealth.

Environmental groups have been quick to support business's view of climate change. After all, the refrain goes, if even business believes global warming is happening then it must be true. According to Professor Fritz Böttcher of the European Science and Environment Forum – a group of scientists sceptical of the apocalyptic pronouncements – 'the "scare-them-to-death" approach has always been a legitimate form of argumentation' for insurers.

Global warming theory is not supported by the data and as a consequence we can't yet know that climate disasters are becoming worse and more frequent. All we can be certain of is that we are spending more time measuring them, and, with modern communications, hearing about them.

35 Government doesn't do science well either

Wall Street Journal Europe (13 August 1996)

If state funding of scientific research promotes success, why does science in Japan and Switzerland flourish in its near-absence, while Russian and Indian science stagnates in a sea of government largesse? This question deserves to be answered, but would never cross the mind of most university researchers in Europe, even as they complain that their research is inadequately supported.

As Terence Kealey explains in his highly entertaining book, *The Economic Laws of Scientific Research* (1996, Macmillan), science is a nationalized industry. Like other state-run organizations, most of its employees prefer to discuss tinkering at the edges of government support rather than contemplating wholesale privatization. They cannot imagine a world without government research councils and state initiatives. They do accept that business can support applied research. But they argue, with almost universal support from commentators the world over, that the private sector wouldn't sufficiently fund pure research on its own. After all, where's the profit in it?

Dr Kealey slowly chips away at this defence of nationalization, by both theoretical argument and numerous case histories from ancient Egypt to modern Japan. Dr Kealey's theoretical approach is based on three 'laws' of scientific research: all countries spend more on research as they get wealthier; public and private funding of research displace each other; and public funds displace more research than they fund themselves. The bottom line according to Dr Kealey is that government support of research hinders scientific discovery.

But false conventional wisdoms generally require history as well as theory to overcome them.

By bringing empirical evidence to the economics of science, Dr Kealey does what Nobel Laureate Ronald Coase did for economics generally when he explained that the textbook example of a 'public good' requiring government provision – the lighthouse – had in fact been provided privately by entrepreneurs who were allowed to charge a levy at the local ports for their service (see Article 16 of this book).

Dr Kealey, who is a biochemist at Cambridge University, is a master of history. In the first few chapters he demonstrates how *dirigisme* suppressed innovation in the early bureaucratic societies of Egypt and Rome whereas the supposed chaos of the Dark Ages led to such advances as the horseshoe, the horse collar, the stirrup, the water mill and even soap. He then moves onto more familiar territory: the Enlightenment and Industrial Revolution. One

French government after another centralized research and funding with little to show for it. *Laissez-faire* Britain meanwhile produced the Industrial Revolution.

The key point that Dr Kealey makes is that new technology usually develops from old technology and not from basic scientific research. The desire to understand what technologists have discovered leads to the demand for scientific research. Papin's theory of vacuums came entirely from studying the steam engine developed by Newcomen. Indeed, Newcomen was completely ignorant of basic physics theory, as were most of the main inventors of this period.

Through numerous examples Dr Kealey shows that industries are the best at developing new technologies out of old ones. Modern Japan has been successful because its private sector copied and then built on old technologies, not because its academics developed new theories. After all, Dr Kealey explains that in a recent American survey, university-based science provided less than 10 per cent of the number and 1 per cent of the value of new inventions. The rest came from those trying to improve existing technologies.

However, companies do invest in basic research, as do charities and individuals, in their desire for publicity, prestige and also to forge links with universities – a source of future researchers. Dr Kealey claims that this would rapidly expand if government stopped funding science. Removing government funding of basic research would not lead firms to immediately endow huge sums to basic research, but the wealth creation they generate will allow natural curiosity that probably would. At least, that's the lesson of the last 2000 years.

The argument for removing government from scientific research is not, therefore, an argument against science but against the stultifying atmosphere of university research environments.

One further problem with centralized research is the way that it can be used to provide support for a position taken by particular government departments or bureaucratic agencies, undermining public support for science. Recent examples of this occur in the environmental and health spheres. Instead of research being focused on areas that are of economic value, it is directed to areas that provide kudos to the researchers and a *raison d'être* for bureaucrats. AIDS, the effects of asbestos, nuclear power and tobacco are the politically correct research subjects of the day. The debate on climate change that took place recently at the UN conference in Geneva was also hostage to bureaucratic and government interference. Although it is becoming obvious that scientific reports are unduly affected by political influences, most of the scientists themselves cannot speak out for fear of losing their funding. Most of those who blow the whistle are either retired, independently funded, or both.

Thus Dr Kealey's book is not only remarkable, but courageous. He has been universally derided for his views and castigated by many of his colleagues for endangering their funding base. It is the first book by a practising scientist to challenge the orthodoxy for decades and should be read by those who are involved in science or merely wish to promote it.

36 The Marlboro Man can't make you smoke

Wall Street Journal Europe (15 January 1997)

Last week's announcement that Belgium will ban tobacco advertising and event sponsorship starting in 1999 follows hot on the heels of Turkey's ban, effective last month. Both these moves are likely to increase the pressure for an EU-wide prohibition despite the mounting evidence that shows that advertising bans do not reduce smoking. They do, however, cost jobs and would limit the development of safer products. So before these concrete losses are accepted, the proponents of bans should produce more than speculative evidence that fewer people would smoke as a result of these measures.

Norway and Finland have prohibited tobacco advertising for many years, yet total smoking has not changed in the former and increased slightly in the latter country. The UK, Belgium and the Netherlands, which have allowed more advertising in recent decades, have seen a decline in smoking over the same period. Indeed, there has been a 28 per cent reduction in smoking in the past fifteen years in Belgium, some of which may be attributable to the banning of image (not brand) advertising such as the rugged Marlboro cowboy eight years ago. So it appears that the relationship between advertising and tobacco consumption is not straightforward.

A new volume of reports, *Advertising and Markets* (1996), compiled by the UK-based business publisher NTC, addresses this complex relationship and explains why bans may be ineffectual or even counter-productive. Conventional wisdom (possibly the result of boastful claims from the advertising industry) is that advertising can easily create demand for products from a naive public. It is therefore assumed that an advertising ban will reduce demand for the same products.

But, as much of the analysis in *Advertising and Markets* shows, advertising is less effectual than is commonly thought. In fact, for mature markets like tobacco, advertising is unlikely to increase total demand, but can induce existing smokers to switch from one brand to another. According to the contributors in this compilation, a ban on advertising would therefore not reduce total demand, but would reduce the likelihood of consumers switching brands. Advertising has been allowed in Turkey and Belgium, for instance, and while there has been a decline in smoking, some brands which are heavily advertised, such as Marlboro, have had an increase in their market share. In Turkey, US and British companies, through massive advertising campaigns, have taken at least 25 per cent of the market from Turkish brands. Despite counter-examples such as these, many people, and more importantly many politicians, tended to accept the idea of prohibiting advertisements because they believed that it would discourage young people from starting to smoke. The Joe Camel cartoon character used in R.J. Reynolds tobacco advertisements are alleged by many anti-tobacco groups to have encouraged young people to start smoking in the USA. A paper in the *Journal of the American Medical Association* reported that Joe Camel was as familiar to six-year-olds as Mickey Mouse. Among high school students 98 per cent recognized the character, compared with 67 per cent of adults. However, the UK government report on the Camel advertisements said that the evidence on consumption is not sufficient to establish that the campaign does actually cause more youths to start smoking. Richard Mizerski, head of the school of marketing at Griffith University in Brisbane, Australia, measured the effect of children's recognition of cartoon trade characters, including Joe Camel, on product recognition in a sample of youngsters: 'The increasing recognition of the Joe Camel trade character tended to be associated with disliking, not liking, cigarettes'. This and other studies suggest that children know that tobacco is bad for them.

A 1991 survey conducted by the EU of 9312 young people in twelve member states showed that peer group pressure accounted for over 60 per cent of the reasons given for smoking, whereas advertising accounted for at most 1.5 per cent. A more recent German study by the Deutsche Institute shows that even the low figure of 1.5 per cent cannot explain why some youths begin smoking: 'Only when juveniles become regular smokers do they become aware of ads for tobacco products . . .' the report said.

It also makes sense psychologically that young people are more attracted to forbidden fruit. The more smoking is seen as taboo, whilst remaining a legal product, the more likely teenagers are to actually try it. Indeed, the most alarming increases in smoking in Finland (and the only increase in the UK) come from young people, especially young girls. Since Finland's advertising ban in 1979, under-eighteen smoking has increased by 7 per cent.

Today's teenagers grow up bombarded by advertising and they become astute at a very young age at any attempted manipulation and in discerning what is and what is not an advertisement. I would venture that seeing teen idols, such as the supermodel Kate Moss, smoking is far more important than any advertisement. Real-life association of smoking with young idols, such as sports stars, including sponsorship of sporting teams, is more likely to encourage smoking than bland brand advertising. And since image advertising has been banned in most European countries, brand advertising dominates.

One reason, considered by several authors in *Advertising and Markets*, that smoking has declined in countries that have allowed advertising may simply be that all adverts now have to carry health warnings. Banning advertising removes this regular reminder that it is harmful. Where restrictions exist, as in most EU countries at the moment, tobacco companies are in a catch-22. Every advert they run reminds customers that their products are harmful, but if they don't advertise they will lose market share to their competitors.

An ironic and unhealthy side-effect of a prohibition on tobacco advertising could well be a slowdown in the development of less toxic products. Over the years, smokers have realized that tobacco is harmful, brand competition has attracted them to lower tar cigarettes, and before that to filter-tipped cigarettes. Without advertising, these products would have been less successful and more people would still probably be smoking higher tar non-filter-tipped cigarettes. Today, with greater social pressure on smokers, some manufacturers are attempting to design cigarettes that have minimal effect on non-smokers. The reduction in side-stream smoke from a cigarette would be a useful selling point in brand competition but without advertising no company could successfully bring this kind of product to the market.

There are also financial reasons to think that restrictions may be better than an outright ban. According to a recent study from consultants at KPMG, the loss of tobacco advertising due to Belgium's ban will cost the advertising network (agencies, billboards, press) about $70 million, and over 250 jobs. The knock-on effects in other related markets (suppliers to these industries) could raise the total cost to $100 million and nearly 400 jobs. The impact of banning tobacco sponsorship of all sporting and cultural events in Belgium will be even more dramatic.

Bernie Ecclestone, head of motor racing's Formula One, explained that without tobacco sponsorship the future of Spa Francorchamps as a grand prix venue in Belgium is threatened. Last year the four days of the Belgian Grand Prix brought in over $35 million of overseas money to the event organizers and surrounding businesses. Because of the revenue, many countries are competing for the chance to host grand prix, in other words, the loss of one European venue will not be missed. If tobacco logos cannot be shown in Spa they will be shown in another country. Consequently, the local Walloon government will lose substantial tax revenues and is petitioning Belgian authorities for an exemption to the advertising ban for the grand prix event. The ban will lead to other sports sponsorship losses estimated by KPMG to be in tens of millions of dollars.

Belgium has had the greatest percentage decline in smoking in the Western world in recent years. Many politicians are aware of these arguments and know that an advertising ban will not make this happen any faster, but to oppose it is to be labelled pro-tobacco, a poisoned political chalice. Belgian Health Minister Marcel Colla has waffled on the issue. In June 1996 when there was a debate on the ban in parliament he said, 'there actually doesn't exist any scientific proof linking advertising and consumption of tobacco'. Nevertheless Marcel Colla supported the position of his Flemish Socialist Party member, Mr Van Veldhoven, who promoted the advertising ban bill. In Turkey a similar bill was passed with less than 7 per cent of the members of parliament present for the vote.

Belgian politicians, even those who were against the ban in their own country, are sure now to lobby harder for an EU-wide ban. They will wish to level the playing field for their citizens who will lose out once the Belgian ban is enforced.

However, the only way to be sure that the politicians in EU countries are serious about the health effects of tobacco would be when they remove the $1.2 billion EU subsidy to tobacco production, and not if they bring in an advertising ban. For the moment tobacco advertising legislation may be politically expedient, but it does not reduce smoking.

37 Fuel fossils: extinction exaggerated

Financial Times (25 January 2000)

The last quarter of the twentieth century has seen numerous green scares: alarming rates of species' extinctions, acid rain, cancer from pesticides, overhead power lines and mobile phones. Most of these have remained scares, based on preliminary research and a readiness to believe them. Good science takes time, and an 'all clear' message rarely has the impact of a 'be afraid' message, so scares stick in the public mind long after they are refuted by science. In this vein, and in honour of the second anniversary of the death of the economist Julian Simon, I will try to lay a persistent old chestnut to rest: The world is not running out of oil.

Well over a decade ago, Simon forced environmentalists to concede that commodities from the earth were in plentiful supply. He did this by winning a bet with the doomsayer, Paul Ehrlich, that any six commodities Ehrlich chose, would decrease in price over ten years.

Given similar prediction failures over fossil fuels, by the 1980s the green machine searched for an alternative but related issue for us to worry about. And so attention has focussed on the potential harm from global warming due to the increased burning of the fossil fuels they said we would have run out of in the 1980s.

Nevertheless belief in the finite limit of oil has remained bubbling below the surface of all debates on alternative energy. Few respectable commentators will say outright that alternatives are necessary because of oil depletion, but they do imply it in their assumption of the inevitability of adopting so-called renewable energy from wind, solar and tidal sources. But the reality is that we will never deplete our stocks of fossil fuels and we must remove the implicit support the depletion myth gives to uneconomic technologies promoted by, and for the benefit of, environmental interests.

World oil reserves are 15 times greater than they were when record keeping began at the end of the second world war. Similarly, gas and coal reserves have also risen by significant amounts. Proven world reserves of coal, oil and gas are respectively 230, 43 and 63 years, at current rates of consumption. Probable reserves are respectively 1,884, 114 and 200 years, says the authoritative World Energy Outlook. But even these figures underestimate the amount of non-conventional sources of fossil fuels that exist. For example, according to Robert Bradley, President of the Houston-based Institute for Energy Research, Orimulsion has become the fourth fossil fuel in the past few years. Orimulsion is a tar-like substance that can be burned to make electricity or refined into petroleum. Technology was too primitive and polluting to make Orimulsion of much use until the mid-1980s but since then it has been used in Germany, Italy, Denmark and Lithuania, and Latin America. The known deposits of the tars used in Orimulsion are vast. Venezuela's are the equivalent of 1,200 billion barrels of oil, larger than all known oil reserves in the world. Even the environmental costs are receding because, according to Bradley, the 'post-scrubbing' characteristics (those that reduce and remove emission of pollutants) of new Orimulsion burning technologies are now superior to those of conventional oil. So as Bradley explains Orimulsion 'represents an abundant backstop fuel at worst and a significant extension of the petroleum age at best'.

Other natural compounds, such as tar sand and shale oil, are, according to Michael Lynch of the Massachusetts Institute of Technology, likely to make 15,000 billion barrels of fossil fuel available in the next few centuries. Couple this with new technologies which have lowered exploration costs by 40% in the past decade, making exploration in previously unprofitable areas worthwhile, and another 6,000 billion barrels of oil will be made available, says Lynch. In short, abundance is increasing by every measure that counts in the real world, and only geopolitical instability, or falling prey to green demands, will stop it. Recent oil price increases from an all time real price low in early 1999 of $10 a barrel to $25 are due purely to OPEC voluntary restrictions.

Furthermore, as the inspirational Julian Simon explained, the only true limits are set by man's ingenuity and while that can be exercised over energy provision, we will always overcome trivial difficulties, like supply, in the next century or two. As Bradley explains 'there is no reason to believe that energy, as opposed to particular energy sources, will grow less abundant'. In other words 'depletion' is not an operable concept for the world energy market, where it is for a particular oil field or coal deposit. Bradley, a prescient thinker on energy issues, considers that in the real world of politics the time horizon is too short, and technological and economic change is too uncertain, discontinuous and open-ended, for information about fossil fuel reserves to have any impact on policy.

The idea of optimal depletion is a useful pedagogic device, a bit like 'perfect competition' or 'Pigovian/environmental taxation', but it has virtually no practical relevance for businessmen or politicians, except in its ability to scare and cajole society into accepting unnecessary policies for the development of 'alternative fuels'. For example, the climate change levy, a UK fossil fuel tax levied on business in the hope of limiting global warming, will raise over a billion pounds a year. Since fuel demand is inelastic and the UK's contribution to world emissions is tiny, the impact of the tax on warming will be virtually non-existent. But as some of the tax revenue will subsidise uneconomic solar and wind power development, and environmental research into green alternatives, its proponents still think the tax worthwhile. And this is a proposition that many people subscribe to. Governments, of course, win twice in that they are seen to be acting on the environment and gaining extra revenue.

However, evidence from the Cato Institute in Washington DC suggests that renewables, especially solar, have an interesting role as a 'bridge' fuel, but are unlikely to be the fuel of even the middle term future. Developing countries that cannot afford large electricity grid systems are looking to solar and nuclear as potential sources of fuel for dispersed geographical locations. However, once the wealth of a country increases, infrastructural grid systems will develop, following a similar, but cleaner, fossil fuel path that the older developed countries have taken. These countries have developed a fossil fuel mix, which has moved from high carbon/low hydrogen content (coal) to low carbon/high hydrogen content (gas), it is far more likely that this ratio will continue to move until we are burning hydrogen only, the only by-product of which is water.

Only time will tell whether man-made global warming proves to be a problem, but given that environmentalists' prediction records are far worse than even city economists, it seems unlikely. In any case, the future for fossil fuels appears secure, since the alternatives simply do not generate enough energy at a reasonable cost.

38 A tax scheme from the apartheid handbook

The Wall Street Journal Europe (31 May 1999)

In the five years since the fall of apartheid, South African President Nelson Mandela has succeeded in keeping his country from disintegrating into conflicts between racial groups and vested interests. But the honeymoon is long over. Serious potential for unrest exists in many black communities where unemployment rates are often over 50 per cent and residents sit idle.

Creating jobs for these people will be the chief task of Thabo Mbeki, who is almost certain to replace Mandela following general elections this Wednesday. Unfortunately, as Vice President, Mbeki has been quick to back job creation schemes that are woefully inadequate and, in some cases, blatant power grabs.

Typical of such schemes is a proposal advanced by Guy Preston, special adviser to the minister of water affairs, to finance a jobs programme by placing a surcharge of 10 per cent on all water used in mostly urban areas occupied by white South Africans. Few blacks live in the areas being targeted with most still living in fringe areas and 'townships'. Township dwellers have rarely paid for the water they use because they did not have good quality piped supplies and in any event, non-payment was a major form of protest in the apartheid years.

Preston also wants to slap a 5 per cent surcharge on water used by the industrial sector. The new taxes, it is claimed, will raise $500 million, which will be used to employ 150,000 disadvantaged black people in government make-work jobs.

Presumably, these jobs will be similar to those that have already been created under pilot projects launched by Preston's so called Working for Water programme. Specifically, 42,000 South Africans have already been hired to mow down weeds, purportedly because they are alien to the South African ecosystem. Preserving South Africa's indigenous ecology is a fine ideal, but is this what the country really needs? Surely this is not the kind of sustainable jobs market that Mandela had in mind when he came to power five years ago. The finance ministry, to its credit, has questioned Preston's scheme, but there has been little objection from Mbeki.

Under normal circumstances, South Africa's white urban interests would rightly complain that this tax is purely about redistribution of wealth. The mostly white Hermanus district near Cape Town is already suffering from massive water tariffs imposed under the pilot project. But to assuage uncooperative whites, Preston, probably with help from Mbeki, plans to sell the idea as an ecological tax. His thinking, which is likely correct, is that white South Africans, who have championed national wildlife areas and other conservation efforts, will support the water tax rather than risk being seen as anti-environment.

But this tax is obviously not about conservation. Urban and industrial entities use at most around 20 per cent of South Africa's total available water. The rest is primarily used by the agricultural and forestry sectors, which pay next to nothing (or in some cases nothing at all) for their water. If conservation were even partly the aim, then any water surcharge should surely be targeted at these groups.

But Preston knows that farmers' demand for water is highly price elastic – they buy less water as taxes go up. Therefore, Mr Preston can hire a lot more weed whackers by hitting urban whites, rather than farmers, with new surcharges. And the more money that flows in, the more influence Preston retains in the water ministry. In addition, farmers are not a soft political target. They are an organized interest group that employs large numbers of (mainly black) South Africans and would be unlikely to give in to Mr Preston s make-work scheme.

Although Preston proselytizes about the 150,000 jobs his scheme may create, he dismisses as 'small' the chance that South African industry will offset the higher water tariffs by laying off even more employees. But, as industry leaders have pointed out, the chance of such job cuts is actually quite large. Meanwhile, Preston completely ignores the fact that urban water users faced with a new tax would lose purchasing power and therefore buy fewer of the goods that people are employed to make.

Clearly, it is folly to tax the rich to pay for an expanded bureaucracy that will only administer relatively insignificant jobs entailing tasks that are already grossly over-manned. Preston's plan is based on economic logic that has demonstrably failed wherever it has been tried around the world. In Africa especially, such schemes have typically only served to prop up ruling elites. Meanwhile, economies continue to stagnate and poverty remains entrenched. Unfortunately, Preston's approach has been unexceptional in the new South Africa. The resulting unemployment and economic decline have left the country in a precarious position. It has survived the stupidity of apartheid without much bloodshed, but accelerating joblessness is threatening the relative peace. In itself, Mr Preston s plan won't condemn South Africa to join the ranks of Africa's many basket cases. But along with similar schemes being touted by the current government, it is certainly a step in that direction.

One ray of hope in the current government is finance minister Trevor Manuel, who is opposed to the Preston scheme, partly because it might scare off foreign investors. The finance minister, while no ardent free marketer, knows that a future South Africa must avoid becoming a playground for irresponsible economic thinkers. As the nation's next president, Thabo Mbeki will have to decide whether to take advice from people like Manuel or from the likes of Preston. For the sake of South Africa, let's hope he makes the right choice.

39 Canada leaves Greenpeace red-faced

The Wall Street Journal Europe (22 July 1999)

It's official: Greenpeace serves no public purpose. No less a Green haven than Canada just dealt the Dutch-based environmentalist group a massive blow to its credibility and fundraising efforts by denying it the charitable status it had sought for a decade. Revenue Canada, the tax-collecting arm of the government, has refused to recognize the new Greenpeace Environmental Foundation as a charity, saying its activities have 'no public benefit' and that lobbying to shut down industries could send people 'into poverty'.

By doing this, Revenue Canada has performed a useful service. Its decision has sent a strong signal to the world's Green pressure groups that their tax and other benefits resulting from their status as 'charities' deserve reconsideration. Canada is the first country to implicitly recognize Greenpeace as the most successful of the multinational anxiety corporations. The question would probably not come up in the USA, where it's comparatively easy to register as a charity. But with regards to Europe, where charity registration is often similar to that of Canada, it's alas unlikely that any European country will have the guts to follow Canada's lead.

Greenpeace was launched in Vancouver nearly thirty years ago with an anti-nuclear, 'Don't Make a Wave' campaign. It was registered as a charity in 1976. Since then it has grown into a multinational, multi-million dollar operation devoted to promoting Green causes around the world. But in 1989, Greenpeace lost its Canadian charitable status amid concerns that it was not a true charity – i.e., it was not providing a discernible benefit to the public. As such, Greenpeace was no longer able to claim tax exemption on its revenues and donors could not claim deductions, which resulted in some donors switching to real charities that did give tax breaks.

The organization responded by setting up the Greenpeace Canada Charitable Foundation, legally (though not really functionally) distinct from Greenpeace. But according to court records made public in June by John Duncan, the Reform MP from British Columbia, the federal charities division found the charity foundation's activities 'have not complied with the law' on charitable organizations.

'This opinion resulted from an audit which raised serious concerns about the charity's compliance with the Income Tax Act. The audit revealed that the charity had failed to devote all its resources to charitable activities', Mr Duncan said recently in a public statement. Of particular concern were the financial links between Greenpeace International and Greenpeace Canada. Hundreds of thousands of dollars were transferred between the organizations, which may violate Canadian laws on charitable activities. Officials were also concerned because the charity appeared to be a fund-raising conduit for Greenpeace, which is not permitted in Canada.

Consequently, the second Greenpeace venture lost its charitable status in 1995. The group launched a court appeal, which was dismissed in September 1998. But by then a new charity called the Greenpeace Environmental Foundation had sprung forth like the regenerated head of a hydra. Revenue Canada called the latest charity 'a convenient way to avoid the consequences' of its past troubled charities and refused to register the group. Greenpeace appealed against the decision but the court challenge ended recently.

Revenue Canada explains that preserving the environment is recognized as a charitable activity, but that the Greenpeace foundation does not qualify because its stated purpose is 'public awareness'. According to a spokesman from Revenue Canada this poses a problem since 'we have no evidence that the distribution to the public of a pamphlet on, for example, the destruction of forests (along the Amazon or the BC [British Columbia] coast) or on the various pollutants emanating from smokestacks has any measurable impact on the environment'.

However, it is widely believed that the decision against Greenpeace had more to do with its extensive lobbying against Canadian forestry exports than Revenue Canada's 'Public Awareness' issue.

Without charitable status, Greenpeace cannot offer tax receipts to its donors. The Canadian Greenpeace Charitable Foundation is already running at a loss (over $250,000 in 1996–97 and slightly less last year), and non-tax exempt donations will be harder to come by in the future.

Greenpeace made light of the Canadian decision however: 'I don't think Greenpeace is going to be made a charitable organization, and we seem to be doing OK without charitable status', said Peter Tabuns, Greenpeace's Canadian executive director. Tabuns can be sanguine about the decision since the financial dealings described by Revenue Canada suggest Greenpeace's Canadian operations are increasingly being funded from its much richer European operation. Greenpeace worldwide receives over two-thirds of its funding from Germany and Holland, and Canada does not appear on Greenpeace's summary chart of donations (but it does appear on its expenditure chart in recent years). Therefore, Revenue Canada's decision will not cause a big cut in Greenpeace's global coffers.

Nevertheless, Canadians seem less inclined these days to go along with Greenpeace crusades. In an effort to curtail Canada's lucrative logging business, activists placed a giant sign for Home Depot, the US-based hardware giant, in a recently logged area, which they claimed was ancient forest, north of Vancouver. The group then issued a statement calling Home Depot a 'major player in the destruction of the world's remaining ancient forests'. Such rhetoric no longer seems to appeal to Canadians, since donations to the Greenpeace charity fell by 15 per cent in 1997, the last year of published financial records. Furthermore, many politicians who initially welcomed environmental sentiments have since become inured to the scaremongering and have decided not to oppose the Reform Party's anti-Greenpeace stand.

There is plenty of 'clear blue water' between Canada and Europe, however. Greenpeace's European operations are far wealthier and receive the blessing of most of Europe's left-wing governments. Greenpeace has also mounted its most successful campaigns in Europe, where politicians abhor confrontation with pressure groups and try to appease them as much as possible. French attitudes have softened since 1985, when their secret service blew up the Greenpeace ship *Rainbow Warrior* in Auckland Harbour. To be fair, European politicians are not given much support by business, which is becoming increasingly defensive, or the media, which thrives on scare stories.

Such official deference – the assumption that Greenpeace is always on the side of angels – looks more and more out of touch. The recent Greenpeace campaigns against PVC plasticisers and dioxins in Belgian chickens did a disservice to the public in obscuring the scientific evidence and fomenting unnecessary panic. Indeed, such scaremongering harmed the public good and hurt consumers by arbitrarily raising producer costs. It was hard to find a single news story that mentioned the concentration of the alleged contamination – a fundamental scientific point, if the allegations of a threat to human health were to have any validity. In fact, dioxin and other organochlorine compounds may cause cancer when fed to laboratory rats in massive concentrations, but have no observable effect on humans at the actual levels found.

Perhaps we will have to wait for Greenpeace-inspired environmental regulations to cause even greater unemployment and unrest before European politicians follow the Canadian government's example. Environmental multinationals such as Greenpeace should be free to pursue their agenda in a democratic society – but it's time governments stopped giving this particular lobby preferential treatment.

40 Saving the problem – Green job maintenance

Economic Affairs (Spring 2000)

Why would Green pressure groups demand that nuclear waste be buried at the surface, when the safer option is to bury the waste deep underground? Why would lobbyists want farmers to move toward organic methods, when it would mean ploughing up more biodiverse land? The reasons are simple really – there are money and jobs in saving problems. And there are numerous advocacy groups to provide myriad problem maintaining solutions, and to receive money to do so. Until recently these advocates have had only limited success, but in the past few years their access to, and acceptance by, the political process has mushroomed.

According to Dr Frank Furedi of Kent University, nearly 10 per cent of the EU budget is devoted to funding advocacy groups. Furthermore, many of these groups now have an institutionalized role as suppliers of policy data and advice to the European Commission.

Furedi's research (see http:www.esef.org/furedi.htm) demonstrates that official support for consumer activism is based on the belief that these organizations have a privileged access to the public. Politicians and officials hope that their association with advocacy groups will lend greater credibility to their policy making, by seeming to respond to public concerns. Furedi considers that official patronage of advocacy groups represents an attempt to mitigate against the loss of public trust in authority.

So to overcome allegations of sleaze, irrelevance and voter apathy, politicians are co-opting pressure groups to help make policy. But this power-shift has had the almost inevitable corruptive effect. For instance, recent bans on phthalate plasticisers, animal antibiotic growth promoters, and tax increases on energy were all inspired and even designed by activists, and all will create more problems than they solve. The first will lead to more expensive and possibly less safe toys; the second will make meat more expensive, without reducing antibiotic resistance in humans (as alleged) and will produce more organic waste; the last will make British industry less competitive and will shift production to countries with less severe environmental standards, which will produce more greenhouse gases.

Despite promoting harmful legislation, consumer activism has become highly respectable, with a semi-official mandate to break the law. Anti-genetically modified food protesters are often represented as young idealists, even naughty schoolchildren, who are acting on our behalf against malevolent forces of commerce. But in fact, says Furedi, they have the kind of freedom to protest that is usually denied to ordinary mortals. When Lord Melchett, the aristocratic leader of Greenpeace, was recently arrested for criminal damage and theft, he was genuinely shocked by his treatment. As far as he was concerned, his organized and publicized destruction of a farmer's GM test crop, was a 'direct expression of people's power'. As the self-appointed voice of the British people, Greenpeace represented its action as an exercise in 'active citizenship' which 'keeps democracy healthy and responsive'. Melchett's antics have further encouraged an already alarmed section of the British public to jump on the organic food bandwagon, and shy away from any new food technology. The irony of this movement is that the low and variable yields of organic farming not only make the produce expensive but also require more wild lands to be used than conventional farming – further encouraging Green campaigns to protect the remaining lands. A perpetuating vicious circle will ensue, the beneficiaries being the bureaucracy who enforce the new legislation and the activists who demand it.

Furedi believes that Melchett, like many other leading consumer activists, possesses a highly elitist notion of democracy. It is driven by the conviction that if they believe that something is wrong, then waiting for an unresponsive political system to do something about it is a luxury that society can ill afford. Professional protesters assume the moral authority to take matters into their own hands since they are acting on behalf of the People. They believe that their unique philosophical insights entitle them to act in accordance with their ideology, irrespective of its legal implications.

The activists' opportunistic mix of breaking the law one minute, and then appealing to it for preferred legislation the next, represents two different ways of getting around the issue of political accountability. For Furedi, this approach indicates that consumer activists have little genuine inclination to confront the political problems that afflict Western societies. 'As the main beneficiaries of the contemporary stagnation of political culture, consumer activists are far more likely to opt for approaches that consolidate the status quo', he concludes.

The inevitable result of this process is policy designed to exacerbate existing problems. But until the public wakes up to the incentives faced by activists, their 'solutions' will continue to dominate British politics.

Part Four

The New Elite: International Science Bureaucracies

41 Global warming: Apocalypse or hot air?

Economic Affairs (June 1994)

What has caused temperature changes over our recent past? Knowing the answer is vital because climate models predict that man's greenhouse gas (GHG) emissions should have led to a 2° C increase in temperature since the Industrial Revolution. Instead, the planet has warmed 0.5° C in the last century and most of that occurred before the majority of anthropogenic GHGs had been emitted.

A report of some Danish research drew my attention to a possible cause of temperature change, other than man's activities – the sun. Caught up in the global warming furore, I had not considered that the sun could be the cause of our climate changing. The two Danish scientists discovered a very high negative correlation over the last century between temperature change and solar cycle length. The possibility is that as solar cycles get longer, temperature falls. The scientists have not stated that there is a causal relationship – only that the correlation is high – so their investigations continue. However, other research may indicate they are on the right track.

In 1988 the Social Affairs Unit published a paper called *Set Fair: A gradualist proposal for privatising weather forecasting*, which showed up the failures of the UK's nationalized weather forecasting. For example, the severe storm of October 1987 killed 16 people and caused at least £300 million damage. The UK Meteorological Office was warned of the approaching storm thirty-six hours before it arrived. However, the information was only broadcast four hours before the storm hit. The Director of the European medium-range forecast centre said 'We cannot say why our other clients in the Netherlands and France passed on that warning to the public and the [UK] Met Office did not'.

Perhaps more interestingly, the paper highlighted the more diverse weather forecasting techniques in the USA, where private weather forecasting is more prevalent than in the UK. However, there is a UK company, Weather Action, which uses a technique called the Solar Weather Technique (SWT). SWT illuminates the influence of the sun on the earth's climate. These London-based scientists deride the classic meteorologists who claim they cannot forecast the weather when it matters.

> Some 'chaos theorists' think changes in weather type are a result of essentially unpredictable 'flip-flops' between weather states. They are mistaken. The SWT shows that the factors which cause key weather changes have causes rooted in magnetic and particle solar activity, and are predictable.

Like the Danish researchers, the scientists at Weather Action realize that the statistical correlation between temperature change and solar cycle length is far higher than any correlation between temperature change and GHG emissions. They explain:

> The SWT is fundamentally different from atmospheric computer forward projection methods. It does not project the present atmosphere forward but identifies key weather events and weather types up to 11 months ahead in specified time windows to within a resolution of a few days.

They achieved an 80 per cent success rate for their thirty-day British Isles and Europe forecasts. The accuracy of their forecasts was independently verified by risk analysts working for NASA. Subject to further research, they believe they will be able to extend their predictions from eleven months to a few years, perhaps decades.

Weather Action believe their forecasting techniques are the best at predicting extremes of weather and at identifying key changes in climate. This makes it possible for them to sell their services to such diverse groups as the water industry, energy suppliers and even clothing retailers in the UK and Europe. Further research into SWT is likely to follow. Indeed, recent work at the Armagh Observatory in Northern Ireland has linked solar activity with temperature change back over the last three centuries.

But will solar researchers get the further funding they require? Even if SWT predicts climate change better than any other theory, the vast majority of government funding will still go into investigating the potential man-made cause of that change. The reason is simple: If man does not cause the warming, man cannot stop it either. Not even an intergovernmental panel, or any other lobby group, would have the audacity to suggest political action to influence the temperature of the sun!

42 Global warming: Don't believe the hype

Wall Street Journal Europe (11 December 1995)

The world's leading climate scientists stuck their necks out last week when they agreed that global warming is here at last. For the first time the United Nations-backed Intergovernmental Panel on Climate Change (IPCC) stated that the 'balance of evidence suggests a discernible human influence on global climate'. In Rome this week, the UN will present this conclusion to a meeting of the world's governments. It will advise that action to limit fossil fuel use is essential. But is the IPCC overstating its case?

Improvements in mathematical modelling of the global climate have prompted the IPCC to be less cautious in its predictions. Climate simulation models are used to forecast the possible results of change – in this case, the doubling of the amount of carbon dioxide in the Earth's atmosphere. Although still unable to cope with ocean and cloud dynamics, the new models do allow for tiny sulphur particles, produced mainly by power stations, that actually have a cooling effect. The older generation of models used for the first IPCC assessment in 1990 predicted warming of between 1.5 and 4.5° Celsius: the new models reduced the range of increase to between 0.8 and 3.5° C.

The significant point, stressed by the IPCC, is that the inclusion of sulphur has improved the credibility of the models by offering an explanation of the fall in temperature between 1940 and 1970 – a boom time for greenhouse gas emissions. The upshot seems to be greater confidence in the simulations of past temperature changes and the alleged proof of man's imprint on the climate record.

However, as even IPCC insiders admit, this summary does not tally with the underlying research. Dr Keith Shine of Reading University points out the disconnection between report and summary: 'In certain sections we stress the great uncertainties in our understanding of influences on temperature. Then . . . we say we can reproduce the climate of the past hundred years'.

In fact, the mild warming that has occurred over the past century is well within the natural temperature range, and mostly happened before emissions of man-made greenhouse gases had intensified.

According to Richard Lindzen, Sloan Professor of Meteorology at the Massachusetts Institute of Technology, the IPCC has only managed to achieve agreement between the models and the actual observed changes by including 'an arbitrary amount of aerosols' in the models. Consequently it is unsurprising that it obtained a correlation.

Professor Patrick Michaels, Climatologist to the Commonwealth of Virginia, joins the criticism of the IPCC. He considers that even though the new models have reduced the predictions of warming by one-third, they still overestimate warming. However, he is unable to prove his point because he has been 'denied access' to UK government model data. He wonders 'what the IPCC is trying to hide'.

European objections to the report have come from members of the European Science and Environment Forum (ESEF), a group of scientists worried about the information control of the hegemonic IPCC. Jack Barrett, a founding member of ESEF, and a chemist at Imperial College in London, said that the IPCC climate forecasts are totally unreliable as 'they exaggerate the ability of carbon dioxide to cause significant warming'.

All these critics accept that it is a difficult task to write a policy makers' summary. The simplifications required to make the complex subject accessible to advisers and politicians inevitably leads to subjective interpretation of what is and what isn't relevant information.

Nevertheless, according to ESEF's Dr John Emsley:

> the IPCC policy makers' summary creates the serious misimpression that a 'smoking gun' has been found that implicates greenhouse gas emissions as the primary cause of the historical rise in temperature. But there is little underlying evidence to support this assertion.

According to Dr Lindzen this bias occurs because pressure is put on scientists 'to emphasize results supportive of the current scenario [of dangerous climate change] and to suppress other results'.

Since policy makers are not hearing the whole message due to strategic editing by IPCC senior managers, it is vital that counter voices, like that of ESEF, are heard. But at this week's climate meeting in Rome, only the 'consensus' voice of the IPCC clique will be presented.

Given that stabilizing atmospheric carbon dioxide, if possible at all, would take decades (maybe even centuries) and would cost trillions of dollars, we had better get the science correct. This is why Dr Lindzen stresses acknowledging the limitations of the models and providing raw information to policy makers. 'If the science in a few years can no longer sustain these forecasts [of 'dangerous climate change'], nothing will stop the policy', he says. 'They are declaring what the policy will be regardless of the science'.

In 1993, the Royal Geographical Society held a mock 'Global Warming Trial' where it was argued that climate scientists were bringing science into disrepute, due to their exaggerated and unprovable claims. There was no consensus in the trial then. However, the jury may yet return a guilty verdict. 'I think in the long run the IPCC statement will be an embarrassment to the scientific community', said Dr Lindzen. But by then the leaders of the IPCC would 'have long since retired'.

43 The folly of environmental directives

Economic Affairs (June 1997)

As the EU slides towards Economic and Monetary Union, and rising unemployment pressurizes continental politicians into advocating re-employment programmes, little attention is paid to an even greater threat to European competitiveness – environmental regulation.

Yet, for many people in less developed countries (LDCs) such as India, environmental regulation is a luxury they cannot yet afford. The Indian Finance Minister, P. Chidambaram, delivered his second budget at the end of February. He is striving to propel his country towards Western standards of living by making foreign investment easier and by privatizing key sectors, like insurance. But, not surprisingly, his budget contained no mention of the environment; liberalization is the order of the day.

Meanwhile, Sir Leon Brittan, vice-president of the EU, worries that conforming to restrictive environmental regulation could cost Europe the high living standards it has achieved.

There has been considerable attention paid to the EU's Social Chapter – the length of the working week, excessive wage costs and the impact this may have on the international competitiveness of European business. However, few have dared to attack the 'environmental correctness' that pervades Europe's consciousness. Environmental, health and safety regulations alone are already costing German business several times the total wage costs of countries like China.

Making these regulations stricter and stricter will stifle European competitiveness like nothing else before. At a recent IEA gathering Sir Leon Brittan was determined to be upbeat about Europe. He explained how Britain had played its part in Europe's success by exporting the benefits of market liberalism in general and privatization in particular. Even those countries that were fervent supporters of the Social Chapter were actually moving towards more flexible workforces following the lead set in the UK.

However, while EMU and the Social Chapter can be vetoed by individual member states, environmental regulations can be approved by a majority vote. And unlike labour issues, where the rest of Europe is following the liberal UK line, environmental rules are following the least flexible and most costly route, tried by Holland and Germany.

One only has to look at the EU Packaging and Packaging Waste Directive to understand why. IEA Research Fellow, Julian Morris, explains 'this Directive requires that all member states recover 50 per cent of all packaging used and recycle 25 per cent of it by the year 2001. This will almost certainly lead to an increase in use of resources and emissions to the environment, as well as cost Europe about $16 billion a year'. Because even if a potential packaging material is much lighter, cheaper and better but is harder to recycle, it will probably not be used.

But what impact will this increase in European regulations hold for LDCs? When I put it to Chidambaram that the UN Basle Convention on Trade in Hazardous Waste would make the transport of used products prohibitively expensive, causing harm to India's secondary metals industry, he was not aware of the problem. He also admitted that he was not fully aware of the implications of the Conventions he and his government were being 'encouraged' to sign. Simply put, he has too many important issues to worry about to spend time on environmental matters, because at the moment action on these issues is largely restricted to Western countries, which bear most of the costs.

But, while agreeing to Western demands on the environment is a potential problem for less developed countries like India, it is an enormous problem for Europeans. Our leaders are publicly, if not privately, interpreting the tacit acceptance by LDC leaders of first-world ideals on the environment as their genuine approval for our regulation. But this is unwise because it is extremely unlikely that LDCs will act on the environment unless sanctions induce them to do so.

For Chidambaram, and future Indian delegations to WTO, a watchful eye will be cast over all environmental treaties. As Western leaders realize the impacts on competitiveness of environmental directives they will try to export their regulatory folly, to level the global playing field. However, it is certain that India's delegates will not allow their country to be 'sacrificed on a cross of Western green', as one liberal thinker put it to me. Indian action on labour restrictions may well be replaced by a hard line on environmental regulations at future WTO meetings. Before this happens, we in Europe should think about the environmental regulations we impose today that may well price our products out of world markets tomorrow.

44 Rio set the bar too high

Wall Street Journal Europe (25 June 1997)

At the United Nations in New York yesterday, British Prime Minister Tony Blair and German Chancellor Helmut Kohl admonished the USA for doing too little to reduce global warming since the Rio Earth Summit five years ago. Kohl and Blair delivered their lectures knowing that both their countries will hit the emission-reduction targets set at Rio. But the UK and Germany are rare exceptions. According to recent assessments by a number of government energy departments, nearly all industrialized countries are failing to reduce greenhouse gas (GHG) emissions.

The findings come six months ahead of the environmental summit in Kyoto, Japan, which will assess the effectiveness of the 1992 UN Rio Climate Change Convention and consider a European Union initiative to further reduce emissions. But whether the environmental ministers meeting in Japan acknowledge it or not, the convention is already failing. The primary objective, stabilizing greenhouse gas emissions, will not be met, and the signatories are losing interest as they face mounting costs and question the validity of the science behind the environmentalists' doomsday scenarios. And if that weren't enough, Australia, a major emitter of GHGs, may be about to back out of the agreement altogether.

As a precursor to Kyoto, the world's leaders are meeting in New York this week to review the progress made since the Rio summit. In addition to wagging his finger at the USA, Tony Blair took the opportunity to promote a European Union plan to cut emissions below the Rio targets. To show he was serious he announced that the British people would attempt to reduce their GHG emissions to 20 per cent below 1990 levels by 2010 – 10 per cent more than agreed to by the previous UK Conservative government.

Blair's commitment goes somewhat further than other EU ministers, who proposed that a major reduction in GHG emissions of 15 per cent below 1990 levels is to be achieved by the EU countries by 2010. The EU target is an aggregate, with differentiated responsibilities for its member states. Luxembourg must reduce by 30 per cent, whereas Portugal can increase by 40 per cent; Germany must reduce by 25 per cent and the UK by 10 per cent (now 20 per cent, thanks to Tony Blair). But the EU position is not unilateral; it will require other industrialized countries to agree to do likewise at the Kyoto summit.

The EU proposal has attracted warranted scepticism, given that most EU countries will fail to hit the Rio commitment. In fact, Blair and Kohl can afford to be smug only because of the unique circumstances in their respective countries. The UK and Germany will meet their targets solely because of the demise of the UK coal industry and the collapse of soot-spewing East German industries.

There is also not much likelihood that the EU proposal will be accepted by other industrialized countries in Kyoto. Japan will miss its Rio target by upwards of 6 per cent, the USA by up to 12 per cent and Australia and non-EU Norway will probably do worse. According to the Australian Bureau of Agricultural and Resource Economics, the cost for the Japanese to meet the new targets set by Europe would be $10,000 per person. America and Australia also face staggering costs, $2000 and $7000 per person respectively. Politicians from these countries will no doubt use these figures to negotiate lower emissions targets at Kyoto, which would scupper the EU deal and endanger the convention.

But to date, the greatest threat to the convention is the growing Australian opposition. Australia is more dependent on fossil-fuel-based industry than either America or Japan, and is especially reliant on coal production. Australian Prime Minister, John Howard, lashed out at his predecessor, Paul Keating, prior to meeting Japanese Prime Minister Ryutaro Hashimoto in early May, declaring: 'We should never have got aboard this particular truck in the first place . . . and those that put us aboard that truck didn't understand the national interest. The economic implications of remaining on that truck are quite serious for Australia'. And one week later when Howard met Kohl, he threatened to withdraw Australia from the convention unless Canberra's own proposals, allowing greater emissions than many other industrialized countries, were accepted.

While Howard's proposals are almost certain to be rejected by other industrial countries, Australia is unlikely to suffer any consequences should it stand alone. And this will only further endanger the convention, as other countries falling short of their targets contemplate a similar response. According to the national newspaper, *The Australian*, Howard has been briefed that Australia is unlikely to be subjected to any formal trade sanctions for its recalcitrance. Any call for economic boycotts against non-signatories, he was reportedly told, would likely infringe upon World Trade Organisation obligations prohibiting discrimination in trade on the basis of non-economic issues.

Although Howard is leading the charge, more signatories are also beginning to question the convention and its scientific underpinnings. The Australian government did accept the recent report from the UN body on climate change, which concluded that there is a discernible human influence on climate. However, the scientific basis for man-made climate change continues to be undermined by new research from all over the world. And Australian officials publicly expressed concern at the Geneva climate meeting last year that many of the underlying scientific uncertainties in the full UN report had been removed from the summary received by media and policy makers, making man's impact on the climate seem more certain than the data suggested.

The report's summary fails to mention satellite temperature data, which has indicated no warming at all in the past twenty years, nor did it acknowledge that measured surface temperature increases may be simply the effect of urban-based thermometers, measuring increased urbanization. Moreover, concerns have been raised that the peer-review process, designed to guarantee scientific integrity, has been compromised by procedural irregularities. One chapter of the supposedly authoritative scientific document claims support from twenty-two papers not peer-reviewed at the time of publication of the report, again undermining the conclusions that the media swallowed.

Ironically, Norway has joined Australia in questioning the convention. Oslo's frustration is understandable. Norway is one of the greenest countries on earth, but it cannot hit the Rio targets or any future ones. The reason is that it produces all of its electricity from hydroelectric generators, which have no emissions, and therefore Norway has few big emitters from which to wring further reductions. Any cuts have to come from transportation or industry, which make up a small percentage of total energy use. But because all reductions outside the EU have to be uniform, Norway's past good behaviour goes unrewarded. Vegard Vik, economic adviser to the Norwegian Conservative Party, estimates that the cost of the EU proposal to Norway could be even higher than for the Japanese.

Other ultra-green European nations have even tried to fudge their Rio targets. Emission-reduction policies have inevitably begun to hurt their economies as jobs are threatened in energy-intensive industries. Denmark, in particular, tried to increase its baseline figure for GHG emissions for 1990 by over 10 per cent, thereby making it easier to stabilize at that higher level in the future, a tactic blocked by other European nations.

Howard's view is gaining supporters the world over. Even American unions and German coal miners are beginning to realize that climate policies may cost jobs. It is this kind of pressure that may counteract some of the global-warming hysteria and reduce the possibility of more nonsensical targets emerging from Kyoto. Perhaps not publicly, but privately, there will be many people slapping Howard on the back for doing what they lacked the courage or political will to do.

45 Business strategy gives away moral high ground

Norwegian Oil Review, **7**, 1997

Businessmen in Australia, Japan and the USA have been lobbying politicians that the climate treaty will hurt their businesses and lead to job losses, which will reduce politicians' chances for re-election. Therefore, they argue that action to combat climate change should be universal to ensure that it does not materially damage their businesses. They argue, with some justification, that jobs will simply go overseas to less developed countries (LDCs) who will produce the goods now made in the West, but with probably more pollution.

This belief is backed up by several studies. A US Department of Energy study (Ronald Sutherland, Argonne National Laboratories, *The Impact of Potential Climate Change Commitments on Energy Intensive Industries* 4 Delphi Analysis, 1997) leaked last week, concluded that a new treaty would 'redistribute output, employment and GHG [greenhouse gas] emissions from participating to non-participating countries'.

Clever?

This business strategy seems clever at first sight. The LDCs will not sign up to anything that requires action by them in the short run, and the Western business community points to the forecast (disputed by few) that early next century LDCs will produce more GHGs than the Western world. Consequently action taken alone by Western countries will simply lead to jobs moving to LDCs with no long-run benefit for the environment, businessmen will therefore not support the treaty.

This is the strategy that the majority of US business is playing out. They have been effective in getting political support from the US Congress. The US Senate recently approved (with a two-thirds majority) the Bird–Hagel Resolution 98, which basically backed up the US business position as outlined above. It was therefore unsurprising that President Clinton did not show his hand at the New York Earth Summit last month. He would be in a catch-22 had he done so, as any US proposal that met the first condition of Resolution 98 (no exemption for developing countries) would have been unacceptable to the majority of UN member states; while any proposal that met the second condition (no serious harm to the US economy) would have been derided by Clinton's European counterparts.

No moral challenge

However, while the Republicans and American business may think they have the Presidency in a corner, they should think twice. Although Clinton will now find it harder to negotiate and sell to the American people a legally-binding climate treaty, he is still likely to succeed.

So what's wrong with the business position? There are many flaws, but the most serious is the failure to challenge the moral vision from which the greenhouse lobby derives all its respectability and much of its influence. Business is not making its strongest case – that abundance of energy is indispensable to achieving a healthier, safer and cleaner world. The greenhouse lobby's anti-growth policies are elitist, inhumane and unfair, and the whole scheme is based on flawed science. Business is in no position to defend itself against opponents who barely recognize its validity, it must attack on its own ground by asserting its value to man and his environment.

Concessions

What's worse is that business leaders are taking even greater risks with what they are conceding. For example, most businesses and Resolution 98 affirm 'the need for global action on climate change'. They are supposing that political leaders can make a bad treaty good by expanding it, by making it truly global, by forcing its regulatory burdens on the poorest of the poor. They are not being forced off the moral high ground – they've jumped.

Political battles are first and foremost rhetorical battles for the moral high ground. European and American politicians and United Nations bureaucrats understand this all too well, which is why they refer to 'fairness' and 'values'. They know, where business does not, that victory will be determined by the premises that frame the debate and define its terms.

Greens vulnerable

According to Marlo Lewis of the US think tank, the Competitive Enterprise Institute, business opponents of Kyoto have come perilously close to saying that America should not support a treaty needed to save the planet unless the world's poorest countries agree to doom themselves to perpetual poverty. The ironic part of the debate is that it is the greenhouse lobby that is pushing anti-growth policies inimical to the interest of the world's poor. This is an enormous vulnerability which environmentalists take great pains to hide, and which business has been woeful in exposing and exploiting, continued Lewis. By attacking green policies as being unfair, inhumane and elitist, Kyoto opponents could seize the moral high ground, but by continually referring to them as costly, inefficient and anti-competitive they make few friends.

Instead, business concedes the moral premises of its opponents without much, if anything, of a fight. For example, as Marlo Lewis's colleague Fred Smith argues, corporations repeatedly try to win public approval with advertising campaigns of the 'we're polluting less than ever' variety. However, this reinforces the perception, assiduously cultivated by environmentalists, that corporations are primarily in the business of producing pollution (i.e. not in the business of producing goods and services that make the world a better place). Accepting the premise of one's opponent may be a lot easier than advancing an alternative moral vision, but once you concede, however obliquely or tacitly, that your opponent is basically on the side of truth and justice, you are heading for defeat, as Lewis puts it.

No evidence of harm

Action only makes sense if global warming is a serious and imminent threat. Yet climate science pointing to a human impact on the planet, as the journal *New Scientist* admitted last week (19 July 1997), is still incredibly weak, and even more important, there is absolutely no evidence that on balance any change will be harmful or imminent. However, business has conceded the main point at issue, and will buttress the position most of the public thinks they have taken, that business is sly and more concerned with profits than the pollution it causes.

Essentially, business is saying that the Climate Treaty is the flawed execution of a good idea, not that it is an intrinsically bad idea. The greenhouse lobby will make mincemeat of this position. They will say, 'No multilateral agreement is perfect, there are flaws in every treaty, especially one requiring the approval of so many diverse nations. The Kyoto agreement is not a total solution, but it is a step in the right direction, and the developed countries of the world have to lead'. It will be pathetically easy for treaty supporters to make concessions that meet, or appear to meet, opponents' demands for global participation, LDCs agreeing to action in the future or by say 2030.

Language only?

One only has to look back to the Montreal Protocol to see how this happened. The LDCs were given many concessions, including additional time to accommodate future economic growth. Pro-treaty politicians in countries that hold the balance in the climate debate, such as Australia and USA, are already trying to move in this direction. For example, Clinton, at the New York conference said the Kyoto accord must include 'language that makes it clear' that developing country obligations will increase over time, 'and will include binding targets'. He also promised $1 billion in aid that will make it to the political decision-makers of the LDCs, if not to the people of the country – a move supported by Britain and other European countries. The key point is that there are myriad deals done to compromise the current business position, isolating those holding out against the convention making them seem irrational and perverse.

Will harm the poor

To scupper the Kyoto accord, business must, according to Marlo Lewis, be prepared to accuse the greenhouse lobby of peddling poor science; categorically deny the need for urgent action; explain that the treaty will harm the poor; explain why the best societal insurance policy is the resilience of a free and prosperous economy (the fact that the same strength storm kills no one in Florida but thousands in Bangladesh, is not down to luck, good or bad); and finally expose the climate crisis as a pretext for the most audacious power play in the late twentieth century. Business may lack the determination to do this, but unless they do, failure is probably assured.

New ESEF book

ESEF, the European Science and Environment Forum, is publishing its second volume of papers critical of the science of global warming. Called *Global Warming: The Continuing Debate*, it will appear in September 1997 and seeks to expose the flawed science (and its incorrect presentation of certainty) that is the basis for the climate treaty and a major threat to modern industrial society.

A wise man once said if a man believes that he is Napoleon Bonaparte, the last thing you must do is to start discussing the cavalry deployment of the battle of Austerlitz with him. Your collusion will compound his delusion and you will never be able to dissuade him of his conviction.

46 Harbingers of hysteria

Wall Street Journal Europe (24 October 1997)

Ten years ago people in South-east England woke up to what looked like a war zone. The so-called Great Storm left British insurers with a bill for about $2 billion, as winds of up to 115 mph uprooted trees and destroyed houses.

At the time it was thought to be a freak event. But lately, it is being touted by the international media as compelling evidence of man-made climate change. The press now routinely takes abnormal weather events as proof of man's impact on the climate. The headlines reflect these convictions: 'Rain moves north in global greenhouse,' the *New Scientist* asserted; 'Global warming is leading to climatic upheaval' the *Independent on Sunday* reported: and even, 'Ahead: Hot times, rising seas and more killer storms', *Time* magazine contended.

There's only one problem. The notion that man-made emissions of carbon dioxide are causing dangerous climatic events is not supported by any plausible link. Consequently, most climate scientists have been voicing increasing doubt about this very notion. But climate scientists did such a good job convincing the media that there was a problem that even those experts who bother to spend time with reporters can't get them to alter their alarmist approach. For example, last year one cover story in *Newsweek* epitomized the coverage the issue receives. It showed a man walking through a whiteout of a snowstorm with the headline 'The hot zone – blizzards, floods and hurricanes: blame global warming'.

According to Robert Balling, Professor of Climatology at Arizona University, 'there is a lack of theoretical or empirical evidence to support the claim that a warmer world will lead to greater numbers of hurricanes or that they will be more intense'. In a recently published, detailed study, Balling and Sherwood Idso, a scientist with the US Department of Agriculture, found no trend of any sort in the number of hurricanes experienced with respect to variations in temperature. Moreover, similar research from Germany's Max Planck Institute shows a global decrease in frequency and severity of storm events over the past forty years.

Balling also claims that recent evidence points toward a future of fewer and less intense hurricanes, if warming does occur. But the media have shown little interest in this kind of research. Balling spent an hour advising *Newsweek* journalists ahead of the 'Hot zone' story, and he insists that their alarmist representation of the facts was not a matter of confusion regarding the complex scientific issue. Despite having asked his advice, 'they chose to ignore the facts and present the scariest possible story regarding our future and global warming', Balling said.

But the media need not shoulder all the blame. Politicians, including US President Bill Clinton, have been banging the alarmist drum in the weeks preceding the United Nations climate summit in Kyoto, Japan. Last week in Argentina, Clinton said that global warming will lead to 'the rising of the oceans, flooding lowlands on various continents and islands in the oceans, and more frequent and severe weather events in all continents, including more severe droughts and floods'.

In the end, both the media and politicians are taking their lead from the UN Intergovernmental Panel on Climate Change. The agency provides the best accumulation of evidence in its dense documents on global warming. But even the IPCC is more cautious these days. Its warming predictions in 1996 fell by a third compared with those made in 1990.

Nonetheless, the media remain focused on the conclusions of the IPCC's major report *The Science of Climate Change* (1995). While the underlying data is based on good science, the summary, which is written for the media, is confusing and alarmist. According to it, 'the warm planet of the future will lead to more severe droughts and/or floods in some places and less severe droughts and/or floods in other places'. To paraphrase, the consensus view is apparently that more rain indicates global warming and less rain indicates global warming. Whatever the weather, man-made global warming provides an answer.

Given this preposterous supposition, the media's alarmism and demands for political action to curb energy use become more understandable. But such measures as raising taxes on fossil fuels are foolhardy until a scientific consensus can show that: Global warming is occurring; it is not a natural and inevitable planetary change; and it is harmful. Unless the countries involved recognize this self-evident fact, they will be passing on higher energy costs to their citizens for no apparent reason.

47 The politicization of climate science

The New Zealand Independent (11 and 18 February 1998)

Climate science is about the future. Most climate modellers make predictions with the appropriate caveats, underlining the uncertainties. Others have not been so circumspect. This is how the global warming scare started.

The level of uncertainty in climate science means it can't predict even the direction, let alone the magnitude, of a physical change. Scientists still know little about natural feedback mechanisms within the climate and the myriad variables that these can affect.

Take the example of regional rainfall. Primitive computer models of the mid-1980s predicted metres of inundation coinciding with whole degrees of temperature rise. The picture was of a climate catastrophe. Yet with every improvement in modelling technique, these predictions have become more modest. Metres have become centimetres, degrees, tenths of degrees, and so on. The models still cannot predict past weather, but the genie is out of the bottle.

Global warming is a political issue and, thus, has a life of its own. Climate change has become a juggernaut not only in the policy process, but also in the scientific community.

Despite the shortcomings of economic forecasting, a branch of economics offers insight into the climate change debate. Public choice theory explains why an understanding of the incentive structure facing scientists, politicians, pressure groups and businessmen is important to understanding the political dynamic on a given issue. Although public choice is often ignored by policy makers and economists alike, it has a rigorous basis.

Public choice theory can provide important insights about the actions of all players in the climate debate.

Climate change could affect everyone. However, most individuals are not, nor can they be, directly involved in the policy debate, which is why they remain uninformed.

Those with a direct interest include energy suppliers, other affected sectors such as insurance, banking, transport etc., those whose business is protecting the natural environment, and those with more subtle incentives. The latter include the scientists, the science-led bureaucracies and political entrepreneurs. They are treated less critically by the media and, as a result, their credibility is enhanced even though their motives are not necessarily purer than the motives of those with an obvious financial gain.

Businessmen face clear incentives on climate change. Solar, hydro and nuclear power executives want it to be real, so their businesses can thrive, while oil and coal executives hope that talk of climate change is nothing but hot air. Other businesses have mixed positions but most back the coal and oil position, if not strongly.

Similarly, Green pressure groups can gain kudos and budgets for promoting climate change. Fund-raising is easier in a crisis, and where debate attracts publicity. As US Interior Secretary Bruce Babbitt, himself the former head of the League of Conservation Voters said 'the bottom line for environmentalists is how do you induce people to send money to sustain the movement'. Thus, environmental groups issue direct mail appeals and take out advertisements hyping fears of a greenhouse catastrophe, demonstrating the need for their continued vigilance. If there is no crisis, why do we need Greenpeace?

Politicians have much to gain. Any facing credibility problems at home can become statesmen in the international arena – an arena where they are less accountable for their actions. They can sign treaties their citizens have heard little about, and which will not take effect until the political leaders are safely out of office. Those politicians fortunate enough to represent countries that will meet their emissions targets can score additional green points by acting in the national interest.

Many mistakenly believe global trade to be a zero sum game. They also believe that by demanding urgent action on global warming from other countries they will benefit at home, especially where CO_2 reduction measures are not yet in place.

The above incentives are clear. Yet academics have remained above suspicion, especially in Europe. Objectivity in science comes from open debate, credibility comes from peer review. Scientists' integrity rests on this debate and peer-review process. Anything compromising these precious, if not unique, qualities threatens the public's trust in science's pronouncements. You could assume that scientists would be relatively immune to public choice pressures. While they may be less subject to such incentives than other groups, they are nonetheless human.

Climate change involves a myriad of scientific disciplines, but is dominated by just a few. The most important is dynamic mathematical modelling. It is the one discipline purporting to provide the vision of the future wanted by the media, and the political system.

Undoubtedly, dynamic modelling can be more relevant to policy than, say, palaeobotany, and it has received the lion's share of climate funding in recent years. This is at the expense of other disciplines, increased overall funding notwithstanding.

There is only so much research money to go around.

Scientists must be aware of this fact. If there is less need for their discipline or their research, there will be less money to fund their endeavours. For instance, the Hadley Centre at the UK Meteorological Office exists largely because of climate change and the money it brings in. If climate change were suddenly to disappear as an issue, Hadley might even close, with its multi-million pound annual budget allocated to other research.

The Max Planck Institute in Germany and the University of East Anglia in the UK are two other major European research centres to benefit from climate change. Scientists lucky enough to be in disciplines related to global warming have prospered in the last ten years, much to the chagrin of scientists in less fashionable fields whose work may be of more immediate and likely importance.

More is spent on climate research in the UK, for example, than is spent on cancer research. So those at the mercy of the fickle funder are wise to keep doubts to themselves. All these incentives and reactions are predictable by public choice theory.

Big science, such as big computer models, requires big money. Competition for funding is intense. In this situation publicity and policy relevance help in the scramble for funds. Climate change has both.

Due to their success in capturing funding, many climate scientists' careers now depend on global warming. So scientists, along with business and political players (and the media, another interest group that merits a discussion all of its own) have an interest in how information about climate change is presented. In such an environment formal scientific procedures and peer review become more important, and deviations from accepted procedural norms become inherently suspect.

For the past decade, the climate debate has centred on modelled forecasts and some climate science.

Obfuscation and myth making have flourished. Consensus is now equated with truth. The source of the science has become more important than the content, and peer review has been used as a political weapon.

The issue of peer review is important. It shows the biases inherent in modern science. Scientists often blame the media for exaggerating stories of alarm. But it is not only the media that like exciting, positive results.

Scientific journal editors enjoy the attention that publishing exciting or ground-breaking research can bring. However, those journals rarely carry papers where the findings are negative. This bias has worrying implications.

First, it is likely that the hypotheses to be tested will be conservative because positive results will seem more likely in such cases. More outlandish hypotheses – ones that, if proven, might broaden the scientific picture – will not be entertained.

Second, researchers are likely to select data carefully in search of a significant correlation they encounter on the way. Careers may depend on such things.

Saying that an ice shelf has become larger, tree lines and temperatures were higher in the past, or that uncertainties remain, is simply not good enough to attract attention to one's research.

Prompted by funding applications from US climate modellers in the late 1970s two United Nations bodies – the World Meteorological Organization (WMO) and the UN Environment Programme (UNEP) – embraced climate research.

In 1988, as global warming was becoming a prominent issue, these two bodies set up the Intergovernmental Panel on Climate Change (IPCC). It was aimed at developing a realistic international strategy for addressing climate change and it was assumed that climate change was a fact.

With its assumptions in hand the machine trundled on, commissioning research, holding international meetings in exotic locations and producing a series of reports on the state of climate science and various policy options.

The reports were branded by Massachusetts Institute of Technology Meteorology Professor Richard Lindzen as 'waffle statements which don't say anything. But nobody can disagree with them'.

Things changed with the IPCC's second assessment report in 1995. It claimed 'the balance of evidence suggests there is a discernible human influence on the global climate'. This was seized upon by environmental interest groups, and the media, as final evidence of a scientific consensus on climate change. Environmental leaders claimed it was definitive proof that urgent action was warranted.

However, was the scientific consensus supporting this view politically engineered? Scientists themselves were uncertain. The credibility of any scientific information is important. Most commentators assume that scientific documents are based on science, not politics and, hence, are objective.

It is believed the IPCC provides a politically relevant consensus view because it uses the scientific peer-review process. Everything is read, discussed, modified and approved by a panel of experts. Its reputation hangs on this critical approach, and its adherence to strict governmental review procedures. IPCC author, Keith Shine of Reading University, says the panel's papers are scoured line by line by policy makers. 'They change the way it is presented. It is peculiar that they have the final say in what goes into a scientists' report. The science is scientific, but the spin placed upon it is political.'

A report approved by the world's governments at the IPCC meeting in Madrid 1995 and published in July 1996, included alarmist post-plenary changes that could not be scrutinized. Gone is any meaningful emphasis on uncertainties about man-made climate change. Gone are concerns about unwarranted conclusions being drawn from the studies.

The underlying 1995 report did not state that human induced climate change had occurred. Since July 1996, with no new data to consider, it does.

Certain sentences were deleted from the report: 'None of the studies has shown clear evidence attributing the observed changes to the specific cause of increases in greenhouse gases'. This was replaced with 'If the observed global mean changes over the last 20 to 50 years cannot be fully explained by natural climate variability, some (unknown) fraction of the changes must be due to human influences'. The draft conclusion to the report was also deleted.

The report also included unpublished papers as the basis for its conclusions. For example, Chapter 6 of the second assessment report contains twenty-two references to papers not peer-reviewed at the time of publication. Wider comment on the papers was impossible.

The timing of the deletions and alterations suggests liberties were taken with procedure, in order to achieve consensus. Policy makers, and the plethora of applied scientists and socio-economic specialists, welcomed the IPCC conclusions and glossed over the irregularities.

Instead they attacked industry lobbyists who pointed out the changes. They dismissed critics as practitioners of 'tobacco science'.

The IPCC's indiscretions seem to be rubbing off on its founder organization, the UNEP. Last year, scientists working for UNEP's report on the ozone depleter, methyl bromide, became concerned about alterations to the document. UNEP consultants say the rewritten documents now dishonestly overstate the potential for methyl bromide substitutes.

Climate change document alterations will have a far greater impact. As national officials rely on the exact wording of the reports they sign their names to, the reports should be finished when they are approved drafts. Post-plenary alterations undermine the entire IPCC negotiating process. Government officials will be less likely to approve documents in the future if they believe they will be tampered with after signature.

Breaches of climate treaty protocol were noticed first in the USA, not in Europe. Is there a greater European trust of professional hierarchies? Trust of officialdom and the United Nations may not be high in Europe, but it is far lower in the USA. Perhaps the science debate is less open in Europe than in the USA.

The scientific debate must stay alive, so there is not a premature rush to implement costly policies. Given the pro-warming biases apparent in funding, publication, presentation and in policy, this is vital.

48 Make way for big environment

Wall Street Journal Europe (May 1998)

We are used to phrases like Big Government and Big Business, but what about Big Environment? The bearded sandal-wearing environmentalist of the past is being replaced by the clean-shaven smooth-talking sound-biting environmentalist of today. The environmental movement has big budgets, employing public relations giants like US-based Fenton Communications to coordinate glossy Green press conferences and media stunts.

Not only have environmental pressure groups substantial financial clout of their own, but their lobbying has helped persuade governmental and international bureaucracies to squeeze vast sums from taxpayers to pursue Green agendas. The global warming issue clearly demonstrates this spending largesse.

I recently returned from holidaying in Trinidad which, coincidentally, was the venue chosen by scientists from the UN Intergovernmental Panel on Climate Change to discuss 'Aviation and the global atmosphere'. The scientists' spokesman, Sir John Houghton, has been demanding a tax on aviation to reduce the demand for international travel, which is adding greenhouse gases to the atmosphere. The fact that there are no climate researchers based in the Caribbean, or that more fuel would have been used getting to Trinidad than to London or the east coast of America (where most of the researchers are based) seemed to have escaped the organizers of this meeting. What obviously didn't was that the weather was a lot nicer in Trinidad than in Boston.

The hypocrisy of UN bureaucrats demanding policies which will make people pay even more for their own holidays and the Green elite's trips is simply astounding. For example, gasoline and heating-fuel tax rises in the UK in the name of the environment have already harmed the poor and pensioners, who now use less fuel in winter for fear of the bills. Aviation tax hikes will just be the next elitist policy to come from the greens.

What is perhaps most ironic is that the UN climate dogma is now coming under attack from scientists. Last December world leaders received a letter signed by over 500 scientists who argued against limiting energy use to control greenhouse gas emissions. The signatures, which now number over 900, were collected by two not-for-profits groups – the Advancement for Sound Science Coalition (based in Washington DC), and the European Science and Environment Forum (based in the UK, which I direct).

Specifically, the signatories, who come from twenty countries, urge world leaders not to support the Kyoto accord agreed in principle at December's UN climate conference. They recommend that 'the world's governments defer taking action on a climate change protocol until the science shows limiting greenhouse gas emissions will benefit, not harm, the global environment and public health'. Furthermore, a similar scientific attack (The Oregon Petition) has now been signed by over 18,000 scientists.

But of course the media regularly refer to the famous UN-backed 1995 statement that 'the balance of the evidence suggests a discernible human influence on global climate'. This statement came from a chapter written by Ben Santer in a UN report, which was heavily criticized by Frederick

Seitz for containing 'the worst corruption of the peer-review process' that he had seen in sixty years. Seitz, a former president of the American Academy of Sciences, was incensed that conclusions should be drawn from a report subject to what he saw as methodological trickery. Nevertheless, Santer's conclusions were widely reported. They were based on climate models, one of which was designed by Joyce Penner, then of the Lawrence Livermore National Laboratory in the USA. Penner was also co-author with Santer of the key paper referred to by the UN report. The paper concluded that 'our results suggest that the similarities between observed and model-predicted change ... are unlikely to have resulted from natural internally generated variability of the climate system'.

Penner's new work at the University of Michigan shows that some human emissions cool the planet and others warm it. Her recent press release from a paper she gave in December to the American Geophysical Union, states that 'contrary to conventional wisdom, new computer modelling ... suggests that global warming might not be the product of human activity'. However, no doubt under political pressure, she later claimed that her own press release misrepresented her views.

Nevertheless, nearly two years ago Tim Wirth, then US under-secretary of state, told the UN that 'the science is settled'; yet now that the Green movement has the protocol it wanted, it turns out that this century's warming is probably just due to natural variability.

A further irony is playing out in the business community, for just as scientists are expressing serious doubts over the proclaimed dangers of global warming, multinationals, including some oil companies, are clamouring to show their concern and take action to curb greenhouse gas emissions. The first step for them was to change their rhetoric and for that they turned to environmentalists.

Leaked internal memoranda from the Washington-based eco-pressure group National Environmental Trust (NET) claim credit for opinion articles on climate change apparently written by Enron Corporation's CEO, Ken Lay. From Houston, Enron spokesperson Carol Hensley confirmed NET'S involvement in the Lay story, which was placed in several newspapers by Knight-Ridder. But industry is not alone in calling on NET to write or edit its speeches in order to appease the Green movement. UK Environment Minister Michael Meacher readily acknowledges NET'S help, as did his Conservative predecessor, John Gummer, whose article attacking US business, in the *Washington Post* in December, was among NET'S claimed 'successes'.

Inherent dangers arise from these collaborations. With the debate all but extinguished, regulations and taxes, proposed with the aim of helping the environment (whether or not they have a hope of succeeding) will inevitably be biased towards protecting the large business and political interests involved in the collaborative process, at the expense of smaller, newer companies, the poor and consumers – groups that are inevitably less well organized at placing news stories and at lobbying.

49 Another silly attack on a useful pesticide

Wall Street Journal Europe (19 January 1999)

European Union ministers decided late last month to ban the important agricultural pesticide methyl bromide by 2003. They were following the US Environmental Protection Agency, which is leading the green charge laid down by the blueprint established by the 1987 Montreal Protocol. But this kind of US leadership Europe does not need. Hindsight and scientific advances tell us that the protocol was a vast overreaction and that ozone depletion is not the problem it was thought to be.

Banning so-called ozone depleters has produced no measurable benefit, but it has come at an enormous cost. The UN-brokered protocol was a framework for phasing out all substances that could potentially damage the ozone layer. Aerosol propellants were the first to disappear, then lesser culprits such as refrigerator coolants. Given what we now know, though, the responsible action is to draw a line under the Montreal Protocol and move on.

According to climate scientist Fred Singer, the University of Virginia professor who has invented ozone monitoring equipment, there has been no increase in dangerous ultraviolet radiation reaching the earth. Skin cancers have doubled over the past twenty years because white-skinned northerners burned themselves on holiday in the sun in the 1960s and 1970s. But this increase has nothing to do with chemical emissions and the ozone layer, which is still protecting us adequately from the sun's rays. Consequently, banning ozone-depleters has provided us with as yet no identifiable benefit, but, according to policy analyst Ben Lieberman of the Competitive Enterprise Institute in Washington DC, it has cost upwards of $100 billion in the USA alone.

Nevertheless, methyl bromide will be banned for no other reason than to complete a political timetable. The EPA unilaterally said it was to be banned from 2000, then in October agreed to extend the phase-out to 2005 under pressure from American farmers. Developing nations are reprieved until 2015, but America urged Europe to follow its original target. Northern EU states like Germany wanted a ban from 2001, while southern states such as Italy and Greece were holding out for 2003, which was eventually agreed. The EU environment ministers' decision leaves European users with the same serious problems as American users – how to get along without methyl bromide, and how to compete with other nations like Mexico that will have a methyl bromide advantage for over a decade.

Though the deadline is fast approaching experts agree that there are no viable alternatives to methyl bromide for many of its most important uses, from preparing soil before planting to protecting food against pests during storage, processing and shipment. According to the US Department of Agriculture, 'the likelihood of developing new, effective fumigant alternatives to methyl bromide appears very remote'. Any alternatives are also unlikely to be approved before the ban is enforced.

The USDA predicts the annual cost of the ban to American agriculture will be over $2.3 billion in lost production and higher storage and distribution costs. International trade in fresh produce will also be adversely affected. Methyl bromide is the only pesticide to stop spoilage reliably in long transit. Indeed, Japan currently demands American exported fruit be sprayed with it.

The world's consumers will, of course, suffer higher prices for strawberries, tomatoes, peppers, carrots and several other methyl bromide-dependent fruits and vegetables, as well as the possibility of reduced availability and increased food safety problems.

So much for the costs, but what of the benefits? Some scientists believe that national and international regulators are now chasing after phantom threats. Recent evidence shows that most methyl bromide is created naturally and that most of its molecules harmlessly break down long before they could possibly affect the ozone layer. However, this science will not influence the debate.

Last year the UN Environment Programme was accused by its own experts of re-writing documents, dishonestly overstating the potential for the introduction of substitutes to methyl bromide. A total of twenty-two member scientists of its methyl bromide technical options committee sent an angry letter to UNEP in August 1997 expressing 'deep and serious concerns' that their February report had been 'unilaterally re-written' without their consent. The disgruntled scientists stated their suspicion that the doctored report would allow UNEP to persuade ministers that the world could achieve a 75 per cent reduction in the use of methyl bromide by 2001. The scientists were proved right and now Northern European countries seem to be following UNEP's mendacious advice.

According to one of the committee's scientists, Colin Smith of the British pest control company Rentokil, the alterations were 'totally contrary to everything ... agreed by the experts in the options committee'. Smith resigned in August 1997 from the committee in protest. He alleges that US officials, who had already agreed to ban methyl bromide use from 2000, led UNEP to subvert the report in order to protect the powerful agricultural lobby by forcing the rest of the world to follow suit. Smith considers that the result of the lobbying was the deletion of a significant sentence warning of the 'lack of practical alternatives [to methyl bromide] for [fumigating] dried fruits and nuts as well as spices and processed foods'.

And the Green onslaught will hardly stop with the banning of methyl bromide. The pesticide is the last major political hurdle to agreement on more stringent EU regulations on the whole range of ozone-depleting chemicals, including asthma inhalers and aeroplane fire extinguishers. Austrian officials were keen to see agreement in 1998, while they held the EU presidency, and applied great pressure at the EU Environment Council meeting. Eco-battered business negotiators appeared to see a phase-out delayed to 2003 as a success, and did not lobby against a ban. So a ban was inevitable.

But if ozone thinning was ever a crisis, that crisis has passed without incident. There is no point in banning useful chemicals like methyl bromide. Unfortunately, under UN treaties, such as the Montreal Protocol, the inevitability of international politics carries more weight than new scientific information. Ozone science rarely informs ozone policy, as we undoubtedly witnessed at the recent Environment Council meeting.

50 Growing the Green bureaucracy

Wall Street Journal Europe (January 1999)

The environmental slogan of 'thinking globally, acting locally' has been turned on its head in the 1990s. Irrespective of what environmentalists have been thinking, their only notable successes have been international agreements. Environmental power and influence is shifting inexorably up the political hierarchy. To most, this development is seen as a thoroughly good thing, but there are reasons enough to be extremely wary of the environmental empire builders.

Government signatories to the UN Climate Convention who met recently in Buenos Aires claim they've taken a step toward saving the planet by setting limits on carbon dioxide emissions. The fact that science does not yet, and may never, support their belief of greenhouse-gas induced harm does not deter the bureaucrats from their mission. But not only is the aim of the Convention probably groundless, its side-effects are turning out to be far worse than critics first feared. The emerging concern is that UN-inspired international laws, such as the climate treaty, are undermining national sovereignty by handing power to interest groups and international bureaucrats.

But how has this loss of sovereignty occurred with so few complaints? One theory is of political sleight of hand, where one ingrained anxiety (nuclear war) has been skilfully substituted for another (environmental disaster).

It's certainly too far-fetched to suggest that some kind of supranational conspiracy planned for the environmental agenda to step in when the Soviet Union imploded, although as the joke goes 'throw a socialist out of the window and an environmentalist will walk in through the door'. But the incentives of the 'crisis entrepreneurs', the eco-pressure groups, the old defence bureaucracy and the new Green bureaucracy, ensured that the void left by the Cold War was filled in the public mind. The scaremongering worked because the international community sighed with collective relief when the UN climate secretariat was established in the early 1990s to tackle global warming, as it was then called.

In his 1982 book, *Progress and Privilege*, William Tucker set out the blueprint for bureaucratic expansion of power. Bureaucrats succeed he claims 'by extending the rules of society to cover as many aspects of life as possible'. By controlling emissions of carbon dioxide the climate treaty comes as close as possible to controlling life itself. Carbon dioxide is, after all, essential for all life on the planet, despite being considered a pollutant by the world's regulators. World governments who have handed the climate secretariat power to determine what must be done, are glad to be rid of the moral responsibility. But international bureaucrats' best interests rarely coincide with those of the man in the street, or even of his government.

Margaret Maxey, Professor of Bioethics at the University of Texas in Austin, claims that the whole UN process of bureaucratization could lead to dissolution of independence among sovereign nations. This may precipitate their eventual replacement by a supranational realignment of power. By then, of course, it will be too late to protest that this isn't what voters wanted.

Establishing a treaty is only the beginning of the loss of sovereignty. On acceptance many treaties become legally binding on nation states, yet they are routinely changed years after they were ratified. Such changes are made at the discretion of the secretariat which frequently appropriates greater powers to itself and successful pressure groups. For example, under the Montreal Protocol, ozone-depleting asthma inhalers are likely to soon be banned in Europe – a madness that would never have been agreed by the initial signatories in 1987. But the bureaucrats who banned the major CFC sources are now going after every last emission source. They use groundless fears of ozone-loss induced skin cancer to ensure the ozone issue stays alive and they keep their jobs.

A new book from the Capital Resource Center, *Global Greens* by James Sheehan (1998), details other dangers of the expansion of unaccountable supranational bureaucracies. Sheehan explains that environmentalists and occasionally big business, who have restricted access to politicians at home, have far greater freedom to lobby politicians and international bureaucrats at UN meetings. He claims environmentalists unduly influence many UN agreements such as the Basle Convention on hazardous waste, which seriously undermines trade in scrap metal, and even donations of used clothes destined for the world's poor.

Many Green groups that used to oppose UN and World Bank programmes have now been drawn into the bureaucracy by UN money, claims Sheehan. For example, in 1995 a coalition of Green groups, including Friends of the Earth and Greenpeace, claimed that the World Bank's Global Environment Facility was 'dysfunctional, undemocratic and unaccountable'. Several months later the same groups said the GEF was 'essential to solving critical environmental problems'. The result of this UN largesse and Green hypocrisy is that at last year's Kyoto climate meeting there were 3500 representatives from (predominantly European) pressure groups and only 1500 delegates from member governments. Not surprisingly, therefore, Sheehan cites examples of third world participants at the UN meetings being repeatedly ignored in favour of alarmist 'eco-imperialist' Greens, whose presence at the meeting was larger and more vocal.

Ironically, some Green lobbying has led to regulations that will harm the environment. For example, the Convention on Biological Diversity supplants US regulations on biotechnology products with unscientific and more burdensome international regulations. Henry Miller, Senior Research Fellow at the Hoover Institution, says that such limits will significantly hamper research capable of supplying 'more plentiful and nutritious foods and biological alternatives to chemical pesticides and fertilizers'. The effect – more land goes under the plough, potentially reducing the area of important ecosystems.

Furthermore, the UN World Heritage Sites Convention, supposed to help third world governments protect their natural sites, has wound up being used against Europeans and Americans. For example, the WHS UN secretariat disallowed a mining project four miles from Yellowstone Park because of concern (which was groundless) that the park would be harmed. Montanan businessmen have been in a legal battle for years to begin mining because of the unnecessary involvement of the UN.

The US and EU delegates who recently jetted back from Buenos Aires probably consider they have brokered a good climate deal. And the interests lobbying them at the meeting left well satisfied. But they will have further reduced national sovereignty in favour of an unaccountable bureaucratic elite of which they are happy to be a part. All those who oppose needless bureaucracy should hope the US Congress sticks to its guns and rejects the deal, as it has threatened.

Europe is becoming increasingly bureaucratized and no constituency on this side of the Atlantic is likely to oppose the UN power grab. In fact European politicians seem to be nestling comfortably into their first-class seats on the international environmental gravy train.

51 Global Greens

Energy and Environment (**10**(2) 1999)

There is a rapidly expanding interest in the issue of 'global governance'. With issues ranging from European tax harmonization to international treaties on organic pollutants authors of academic papers and more popular books are finding avid readers amongst the world's intellectuals. James Sheehan's book, *Global Greens: Inside the International Environmental Establishment* (Capital Research Center, Washington DC, 1998) is one of the first to discuss the role that non-governmental organizations (NGOs) have played in this international decision-making process, and certainly the first to be highly critical of their role.

From the beginning of the book Sheehan's forthright prose leaves the reader with little doubt as to his opinion of most NGOs, especially Green ones. He considers that few Americans are aware that environmental organizations, 'an ideologically driven political force staffed by professionals and financed by millions of dollars in public and private funds', exercise real power in the conduct of diplomacy and the creation of international policy. Using international law and assisted by the UN and other international agencies, these groups are working behind the scenes to undermine national self governance, economic freedom and individual liberty. If this continues unchecked Sheehan foresees an ominous future as the last of the central planners advance their global agenda through a professed concern for Mother Earth.

Sheehan's rhetoric will raise the hackles on any environmentalist (radical or otherwise), and he may overplay the power of environmental NGOs at international meetings. But whether one favours or distrusts powerful environmental groups or international agreements, it does appear that a considerable loss of national sovereignty is occurring, and without any public debate.

Historically disputes have been resolved through bilateral contractual agreements or via arbitration involving the countries affected by a given disagreement. The new UN-backed regime evolving under international environmental regulation furthers ventures of international cooperation that try to secure near universal participation. No longer are only a few countries involved in a dispute, it has become a global issue. First of all, this engenders the idea of 'the global commons' where it is possible to conclude that borders are no longer relevant – emissions of carbon dioxide in Minneapolis become the concern of people in Lagos and Ulan Bator. Second, international agencies, created as an ongoing authority are required to implement and direct the details of the global plan. Finally, as borders are blurred there is an expanded role for NGOs to act on behalf of an ambiguous 'humanity' or 'earth'. A detailed discussion of exactly how this process will undermine sovereignty is unfortunately lacking in Sheehan's book, however, it can be found in books such as *Sovereignty Matters* by Jeremy Rabkin (American Enterprise Institute, Washington DC, 1998).

The strength of Sheehan's book is in its discussion of the various UN sponsored international meetings (and the antics of the various participants). Examples include the Rio Summit, the Cairo population meeting and the recent climate meeting in Kyoto, most of which Sheehan attended. Sheehan points out that the various business and environmental NGOs, who have restricted access to politicians at home, have far greater freedom to lobby politicians and international bureaucrats at UN meetings. NGOs heavily influence many UN agreements such as the Basle Convention on hazardous waste, which creates barriers to trade in scrap metal, and other used products. Sheehan shows how protectionist northern business interests ally with environmental NGOs in this type of process.

Perhaps the most interesting discovery from Sheehan's analysis is that Green groups who once opposed UN and World Bank programmes have been drawn into the bureaucracy by UN money and now they dominate UN meetings.

For anyone interested in the environmental community (especially of America), this is a useful reference book. There are over forty pages of tables devoted to explaining who gets money from whom, and how it is spent. It also provides coverage of which people sit on important UN Environmental Committees for key treaties like ozone, climate, biodiversity, forestry and many more. It opened my eyes to how big a business environmentalism has become.

Sheehan concludes the book with the following statement:

> Global Greens have put their faith in the 'process'. They have achieved success even when their ideas have been discredited. What is needed now is the vigilance to detect their manoeuvrings and the skill to overcome them.

Most people, especially non-Americans, will disagree with the idea that the Green movement is harming the world, and needs to be stopped. However, by the weight of examples that Sheehan accumulates where Green groups' actions contradict their rhetoric and create adverse results, it is no longer safe to assume a benign influence.

52 Elites prosper at UN POPs meeting

Novo (October 1999)

While one part of the UN battles to preserve East Timor, another, the Environment Programme, is trying to preserve us all from pollution. Last week the third meeting of the international negotiating committee (INC3) for the Convention on Persistent Organic Pollutants (POPs) neared an agreed text for the elimination of POPs. Next year the final text will be agreed and signatory government ratification will begin. But it will be to no avail. The POPs to be banned are rarely used anymore and don't cause any real harm, despite those imagined by Green groups. The convention appears pointless except that it will achieve the covert aim of its designers – to maintain an international bureaucratic elite.

There has been much discussion of one POP recently, the environmental scourge – DDT. The pesticidal qualities of DDT are still vital for mosquito and hence malaria control, and when I set off for Geneva I was determined to support the use of DDT. As an observer I had no vote or even the right to intervene in any way in the process. But since much of the discussion takes place in the corridors I thought I might try my hand at lobbying delegates.

According to the head of the Malaria Project, Amir Attaran, most of the delegates he spoke to at INC1 (Vancouver, June 1998) were not aware of DDT's use in malaria control, and it's a credit to him and his colleague, Professor Wen Kalima from Tanzania, that by INC3 everyone knew. As a result, an embarrassed spokesman for the World Wildlife Fund (WWF), the NGO which had pushed hardest for the 2007 phase-out date, intervened in the first session to say that they were 'dropping discussion of deadlines' as these were unduly polarizing the debate. It appears that DDT had a stay of execution and my journey was wasted.

Nevertheless, as I listened to country delegates speak at the plenary sessions I discovered some interesting facts. UNEP pays (well, taxpayers really pay) for one delegate to attend from every UN country. For most poor countries, the UNEP-sponsored delegate was that country's sole representative, while the US team sent about twenty delegates, beaten in size by at least one environmental group.

Perhaps more surprising than the size of the environmental contingent was that almost none of the countries represented used the twelve POPs to be banned. Indeed, following Western concerns many said they already had local regulations or voluntary agreements restricting these POPs. Furthermore, better, safer, cheaper products continually displace older technologies. However, to accelerate the evolutionary change from POPS, poorer countries would need financial assistance. I lost count after eighteen countries intervened to support this notion. It soon became clear that if the Northern countries wanted faster change they would have to pay for it.

It was obvious that the Northern countries were driving the process, even drafting the negotiating text without significant African input. This happened because UNEP failed to provide the francophone countries with a French–English interpreter for the African breakout session. Although the South African delegate volunteered to interpret, this inevitably slowed proceedings. By the time the Africans had come up with an agreement, the debate had moved on in plenary. Their complaints and suggestions were left out and may be dealt with at a later stage.

If this was alarming, worse soon followed. No one could point to any scientific papers that demonstrated any real harm from POPs (except for some occupational use, when strict practices are observed). The claim that ambient concentrations of POPs can harm people in a local area, let alone hundreds or thousands of miles away, appears weak, and the latter would be essential to justify an international convention. The Inuit representatives intervened to remind everyone that their body fat contains higher (1 part per million) concentrations of DDT than other Canadians and that this may harm them (though no proper study has found any proof of this). Non-statistically significant correlations between POPs accumulation and disease, from poorly designed studies, was the best 'evidence' anyone had to offer to demonstrate harm. It became clear that evidence did not matter because the *raison d'être* of the convention is the precautionary principle. The possibility that the Inuit or bald eagles *may* be harmed by POPs is enough for the convention drafters.

Of course, the problem of taking precaution as a principle is that it is never-ending. Why ban just these twelve almost defunct POPs listed so far? Many other POPs (there are hundreds in use) could cause 'harm' to humans, since they kill rats at high doses. The Samoan delegate even suggested two more that should be added. But no one was really pressing for further listings because the aim of the process was readily apparent. It was to get textual agreement which would speed the Convention to become law. Listing useful POPs would delay the process, potentially encouraging dangerous debate about the need for the Convention. Currently useful chemicals, such as the pesticide methyl bromide, can be listed once the convention has the weight of law behind it. At that time, veto or non-compliance will be illegal, and the only debate will be over whether new POPs should be listed.

In short the current Convention will protect us from chemicals which don't really cause any harm and that no one uses anymore (except for DDT). Only later additions will actually have a noticeable effect.

But once ratification of the Convention begins it will spawn another global bureaucracy. Besides the administrators, POPs bans will require considerable policing. One can see a future of blue beret POPs cops curtailing violations, perhaps from a factory in Vietnam, in the name of planet earth, with all the participants in the circus benefiting. The developing country bureaucrats will gain kudos by overseeing implementation and administering foreign government donations. The Greens will be happy as they can return to their supporters (ranging from the Dutch Government to the man in the street) and show how they are saving the planet. Intergovernmental organizations such as FAO and WHO are happy because they can apply their expertise to the growing POPs 'problem', and hence increase their budgets and power.

The only losers from this UN process will be consumers and taxpayers, deprived of products and paying for the privilege, and maybe the odd million who just might die from malaria if DDT actually doesn't make it into the exemptions list.

As I left the meeting for the last time I realized that I was wearing the same jacket as the representative from Senegal. We smiled at each other and I began to feel like I fitted in. After all it is intellectually stimulating debating the intricate detail of an interesting legal convention. I look forward to the next few meetings (INC5 is scheduled for South Africa in December 2000, where its sure to be warmer than in Geneva) where we can trade tips on tailors, and the latest scientific speculation about POPs, perhaps over a nice bottle of red wine. To assuage my guilt at least I will not be there courtesy of UK taxpayers, although that can't necessarily be said for the guy from Senegal.

Part Five

Trade-offs Not Solutions

53 Conservation through commerce

Economic Affairs (November–December 1993)

Just over twenty-five years ago the world's only turtle farm, Mariculture Limited, was established in the Cayman Islands by the founder of the Institute of Economic Affairs, the late Sir Antony Fisher. Mariculture set out to raise turtles on a commercial scale – a unique idea, even to this day. The plan was to provide 'conservation through commerce', building on the phrase coined by the conservationist, Norman Myers: 'Use wildlife or lose it'.

Female green turtles lay thousands of eggs in the sand of tropical beaches. The vast majority are eaten by natural predators, such as the racoon. Protecting the eggs over the first few days increases the chances of turtle survival immensely. Mariculture's aim was to collect eggs from a number of locations, such as Surinam and Ascension Island, and give them just such a 'headstart'. The long-term plan was to farm the turtle and meet the demand for turtle products.

Poaching was also a problem, for poachers would often kill the female before she had laid her eggs. Poaching had led to a significant decline, a consequent increase in turtle prices and even more poaching.

The turtle supplies myriad markets. The shell is a sought-after decoration, the meat is high in protein and low in fat, the belly plate is the basic ingredient of calipee soup, and there are over a dozen other uses. Mariculture therefore decided to breed turtles, providing consumers with the products they wanted, maintaining a significant workforce and, as a by-product, reducing both the price of turtles and the incentive for poaching. But the farm did far more. Mariculture conducted research into the microbiology, virology and nutrition of the turtle, as well as engineering designs for keeping turtles in captivity. Among their scientific breakthroughs, perhaps the most striking occurred on Ascension Island. Their scientists discovered that turtle eggs, laid on the beach did not survive for long when volcanic ash landed there. The ash contained a toxin fatal to turtles. Therefore, Mariculture collected the eggs laid on volcanic ash, which otherwise would have died. Eventually collection turned to breeding. Sir Alan Parkes, former Professor of the Physiology of Reproduction at Cambridge University, said of Mariculture: 'This first-ever breeding of green sea turtles under farm conditions is a landmark in . . . the conservation of the species'.

The farm survived numerous crises, and five years into the project the chances of success seemed high. However, what no one at Mariculture had foreseen was the emergence of the environmental movement as a powerful lobbying force. In February 1973 the Convention on International Trade in

Endangered Species (CITES) was enacted by the United Nations. Its aim was to 'establish an effective system for regulating international trade in specimens which were or may become in danger of extinction'. The convention established two categories for endangered and threatened species: Appendix 1, which allowed no trade unless the species were bred in captivity; and Appendix 2, which allowed some trade and required countries exporting species to get UN-approved export permits.

The green turtle was given an Appendix 2 listing. Fortunately, export permits from the Cayman Government were forthcoming. Unfortunately, the US Endangered Species Act, enacted just after CITES, put the green turtle on to an equivalent listing to CITES Appendix 1. California, under-Governor Jerry Brown, made the importing of green turtle products illegal. He commented: 'Some say farming green sea turtles in captivity will bring them back . . . I incline to . . . believe what turtles need is less people . . . depleting their species'.

Jerry Brown's inclination, and the subsequent refusal of the USA to accept turtle products even in transit to other countries, sent Mariculture into receivership in May 1975, the directors unable to fund any further lobbying in the USA. The farm was bought as a going concern, but the new owners could not afford indefinite legal battles either. Finally, the Cayman Government bought the farm and now keeps it as a tourist attraction, with far fewer turtles than at the height of Mariculture's success. Meanwhile, poaching continues and turtle populations are falling, mistakenly reinforcing the environmentalists' belief that they were right to ban trade in the 1970s.

The lesson which Mariculture had learned and which the environmental movement forgets is, as Irvin Naylor, a Mariculture co-founder, put it: 'The only way to really guarantee the perpetuation of a wild species . . . is to perpetuate the species through its own commercialisation' (see the forthcoming book on the life history of the Cayman Turtle farm, *Last Chance Lost*, Peggy and Sam Fosdick (1994), York, PA: York Production Services).

54 Better dead than bred

Economic Affairs (Winter 1994)

In February 1973, the Convention on International Trade in Endangered Species (CITES) was enacted by the United Nations. (See Article 53 for details on its aims.)

The latest CITES meeting has just taken place in Florida. More species were added to both Appendices, and as usual, none was removed from either. As far as I am aware, the only major species to be down-listed from Appendix 1 to Appendix 2, in the entire existence of CITES, is the crocodile, principally because farming of crocodiles has been such a success.

The reason that more species are added each year may simply be that more are approaching extinction. But there may be another explanation: that this is just another case of special interest lobbying. Incidentally, banning trade in any substance, be it alcohol, narcotics or live or dead animals, creates perverse incentives and initiates or stimulates activities such as smuggling and poaching. Hence the ban itself may contribute to a decline in the species, as the most recent IEA Environment Unit paper explains *(Elephants and Ivory Lessons from the Trade Ban,* Ike C. Sugg and Urs P. Kreuter (1994), IEA Studies on the Environment, **2**, November).

The prime movers behind the introduction of CITES and its increasing influence were environmental non-governmental organizations (NGOs). The Environmental Investigation Agency (EIA), the Worldwide Fund for Nature (WWF) and the World Conservation Union (IUCN) are three of the most important, the EIA being the most ardent believer in the desirability and wisdom of CITES.

Like most environmental NGOs, the EIA, WWF and IUCN were formed with the laudable aim of fighting against environmental mismanagement. Vigorous fund-raising for these groups was essential if they were to get their message across. They were highly successful and by the late 1980s had millions of pounds of funding per year. Many groups have offices situated all around the globe, with thousands of employees. Environmental NGOs are booming.

By pressurizing governments and supranational organizations to agree to directives, treaties and conventions with far-reaching environmental objectives, NGOs maintain a high profile and are therefore able to ensure strong financial support. Targets on greenhouse gas emissions, phasing out CFCs or attempting to stop trade in rhino horn and ivory are examples of successful lobbying by these groups. They have railed against governments for not having spent enough public money on resource protection whilst simultaneously presenting stories of impending disaster to scare their genuinely concerned supporters.

The most recent CITES meeting was no exception. The African elephant was placed on Appendix 1 in 1989, even though its population has never been threatened, let alone endangered. Southern African elephant populations had actually increased in the 1980s due to increased investment in protection, which was financed, ironically, by a policy of sustainable utilization of the elephant. Selling hunting licences and elephant products not only provides revenue but creates local jobs. These countries' officials protested against the inclusion of the elephant on the listing but were no match for the NGOs' representatives. They have the appearance of being on the elephant's side, whilst having a continued interest in misrepresenting the future plight of many species. Impending extinction is good for fund-raising.

Many environmentalists are against the culling of elephants, even though attempting to preserve every elephant is impossible and not compatible with the interests of those people who have elephants as neighbours. As Ike Sugg explained in the IEA's recent paper, one environmentalist, Cynthia Moss, is on record as saying 'I would rather see no elephants than elephants being culled because I think that it is morally unjustified to kill elephants'. At the same time, many environmentalists, including former Kenyan Wildlife Services Director Richard Leakey, boast about the hundreds of poachers – often local farmers displaced by governments from their lands – who are murdered every year, in the name of elephant protection.

Until it is generally realized that environmental NGOs are acting in their own special interest, and that species conservation plays second fiddle, they will continue to garner more support than they deserve and exert undue pressure on governments.

55 Sustainable use of wildlife in Africa

Economic Affairs (Spring 1996)

I recently returned from a busman's holiday in the beautiful country of Zimbabwe. One of the reasons for my visit was to witness the changes taking place in rural development. Zimbabwe's wildlife management, a model of decentralized institutions and strong property rights, under constant attack from Western environmental pressure groups, may be about to implode, with no help from the animal rightists.

The Zimbabwean CAMPFIRE Association was established in 1989 when two rural district councils were given authority over their local natural resources, including wildlife. CAMPFIRE is the acronym for Communal Areas Management Programme for Indigenous Resources. It is probably the best model of wildlife management in the developing world. CAMPFIRE promotes natural resource utilization as an economic land-use option in the interests of both conservation and poverty relief.

Because of CAMPFIRE's success, many areas continue to be set aside by rural communities motivated by the benefits from wildlife utilization. The environmental benefit of increasing the area for wild species to roam is that traditional migration routes for animals are being re-established, which aids genetic diversity.

Animal rights organizations, such as the US Humane Society, have consistently misrepresented CAMPFIRE as a means by which wealthy

Americans can get their kicks by shooting wildlife. These groups never show the reality. 'We are not callous wildlife killers . . . we are a people battling to find lasting solutions of dealing with elephants and other dangerous species which are constantly testing the speed of our children and to generate a few dollars to cushion our costs of recovering decomposing bodies of those children whose speed is not good enough', argues Steven Kasere, Deputy Director of CAMPFIRE Association. CAMPFIRE last year made about £7 million from the sale of hunting licences. With next year's Convention on International Trade in Endangered Species (CITES) meeting to take place in Zimbabwe, the stage looks set for the CAMPFIRE programme to get much international media coverage, invaluable in educating Westerners as to the realities of rural African life. It would have been possible to lobby for the removal of the ban on trade in ivory as well. (This began in 1989 when CITES broke its own criteria by listing the African elephant as endangered, when in fact there are more than ten viable populations in Africa.) Unhappily, the Zimbabwean bandwagon has lost a couple of nuts holding the wheels in place.

The Zimbabwean delegations to recent CITES meetings have been headed by Dr Rowan Martin and Dr Willy Nduku, the former heads of the Zimbabwean Parks Board. Both were prominent in putting forward ideas of sustainable utilization to an international audience. With them at the helm at the next CITES meeting, legalizing the ivory trade could even have been a possibility. Both are, however, suspended from their posts at the Parks Board. Their only crime appears to have been bypassing ministerial bureaucracy. The suspensions appear to have an air of permanence about them, with the new head of Parks, Willis Makombe, firmly in charge.

The lack of continuity and requisite skills from the new Zimbabwe delegation at their own meeting will be seized upon by the animal rightists who may derail any Zimbabwean initiative. As if this were not enough, there appear to be changes on the horizon for the CAMPFIRE programme itself. If the temptation to centralize financially lucrative decentralized programmes is all too prevalent in the West, it is even greater in developing countries.

The new Environment and Tourism Minister, Mr Chimutengwende, denied that there had been a change in emphasis, when I spoke to him in December. He was just concerned that 'corruption was potentially a problem' and that CAMPFIRE funding could be centralized to 'aid transparency'. He would not be drawn on whether Zimbabwe would be pursuing the ivory issue at the next CITES meeting but confirmed that Zimbabwe would be hosting the event.

It has to be hoped that the southern African position of sustainable utilization of wildlife and decentralized control of resources will be maintained and even strengthened at the next CITES meeting. Much depends on Zimbabwe, which is rightly seen as the flagship country. If Zimbabwe falters, CITES may fall further into the hands of the animal preservationists who could one day condemn the local communities of southern Africa to an aid-riddled unsustainable existence.

56 Guardians of Eden

Economic Affairs (Winter 1996)

Southern African wildlife experts recently decided to take a radical step in promoting the ivory trade. They hope to convince Westerners of the necessities of trade, through art – by funding a play – as lobbying seems to have failed. I think it may work.

Guardians of Eden – awarded *The Scotsman* Fringe first prize at the Edinburgh Festival in August – explains that containing wildlife in fenced national parks, excluding local people, does not work and that it is essential to allow these people the control and use of their own land and resources. The bulk of the funding for the project came from the World Conservation Union, which paid Nicholas Ellenbogen, a celebrated white African writer and director, to tour southern African countries to see the problems for himself. His passion for the issues is evident: 'It is high time to set [Africa] free, unbottle her and let her live well in the hands of her people, because they are close to her heart'.

Brilliant animal impersonation routines are carefully pieced together into sequences of mime and music that tell the first part of the story – Africa's evolution. The second part of the play is a parable, in which a dying chief asks his sons to envisage different ways of securing their land's future. Moses plumps for Western aid money; Scorpion becomes incapable with drink; and Genius decides to follow the traditions of his people – if they are hungry then they will kill an elephant for its meat and ivory, but as they depend so heavily on the elephant for food and tourism they will do so sustainably. Genius explains that ivory is a valuable resource that, if sold, would enable his people to be fed. At the end of the play the audience is asked to vote for Moses or Genius and their respective plans. Every hand shoots up for Genius. This response occurred every afternoon of the three-week run at the Edinburgh Festival. As one commentator put it: 'First-world spectators have been voting enthusiastically that Europe is a bunch of oppressive bullies and it's OK to shoot elephants for their meat and ivory'.

The controversial message of re-opening ivory trade that has been unacceptable to blinkered Western ecologists was greeted gleefully by these culturally astute and diverse audiences. They were helped by the characterization of the 'opposition'. The audience laughed at amusing parodies of UN aid agencies with telephone books representing forms that needed to be filled in triplicate, and a naive Swiss researcher who, seeing goats, wanted to know what cheese-making facilities there were in the village. She was absolutely horrified to find out that no such facilities existed, the goats were simply eaten. By the end, the audience was eager for Africans to be left alone by ignorant busy-body Westerners.

As I write this column, *Guardians of Eden* leaves for the USA. It will play at the Smithsonian Institute, and for the US State Department, the World Bank, the National Zoo and elsewhere in Washington DC before moving on to New York. The culmination of the trip is the World Conservation Congress in Montreal in mid-October.

The timing of the play is critical. Next summer in their capital, Harare, the Zimbabweans will play host to the signatory countries to the Convention on International Trade in Endangered Species (CITES). Zimbabwe is one of the few countries that allows sport-hunting and sustainable use of wildlife, and is home to the community-based ownership and sustainable use system of CAMPFIRE (see Article 55). Proposals to allow international trade in ivory are likely to be tabled at this meeting, and *Guardians of Eden* might play a part in convincing CITES delegates to overturn the ban. But with the powerful American animal rights movement bribing its way into South African National Parks, by donating anti-hunting strings-attached gifts of $2.5 million for five years, vital support from Zimbabwe's powerful southerly neighbour may not be forthcoming.

It is therefore likely that the play's message will be lost in the politics of CITES. But Zimbabwean wildlife specialist Rowan Martin, the real inventor of *Guardians of Eden,* hopes that the message he inspired will be as well received in North America, as it was in Europe. Most southern Africans are praying that it will be.

57 Trading in rhino horn helps conservation

The Wall Street Journal Europe (26 May 1997)

The United Nations banned international trade in rhinoceros horn in 1977 to save the species from extinction. But now some African countries are proposing that trade be allowed for the very same reason. Revenues from trade, they argue, will fund a better defence against poaching. This pragmatic approach recognizes two critical facts: Demand is unabated and illegal trade continues, despite current conservation efforts.

But it remains unclear whether the pragmatism of these African range states will win out over the shock tactics and hype generated by animal rights groups. The US Humane Society (HSUS) and groups like it have been running a campaign about how wholesale slaughter will follow a lifting of the ban. The US Fish and Wildlife Service, apparently influenced by the activists, recently announced that it would oppose South Africa's proposal to legalize international trading in rhino products (most importantly horn) at the upcoming UN Convention on International Trade in Endangered Species (CITES) in Zimbabwe. The move comes despite the fact that the trade would be regulated and sustainable.

CITES attempts to control trade in endangered animals by placing species on lists called Appendices. The most restrictive is Appendix I, where with a few exceptions international trade is banned. All five rhino species have been on Appendix I since 1977. Since that time, 90 per cent of the world's rhinos have been lost, mainly through habitat encroachment by human settlement and hunting for rhino horn.

Rhino horn is not, as is sometimes thought, sought after as an aphrodisiac but is used in traditional Chinese medicine to reduce fevers. Professor Paul But of Hong Kong University says that rhino horn acts much like a weak aspirin; other scientists disagree.

But regardless of its effectiveness, the underlying demand is unlikely to disappear. Dr Hym Ebedes, a South African veterinarian, says that rhino horn is also culturally important: 'Telling a Chinese person to use aspirin instead of his traditional medicine would be like expecting a Westerner to have acupuncture before visiting the family doctor and using Western medicine'.

According to George Hughes, Chief Executive of the Natal Parks Board, and South African representative to CITES, the current market value for horn is between $1500 to $2500 per kilogram. Hughes joined the NPB in 1961, the same year that saw Operation Rhino, which launched the re-establishment of the southern white rhino to other parts of Africa. Compared with only about twenty animals in Umfolozi Park in Natal in 1900, there are now 8200 in thirty-six controlled areas of South Africa, as well as thirty other populations outside of South Africa.

So while other rhino species have become severely depleted, the southern white rhino has flourished. But rhino conservation is expensive; for every square kilometre of small fenced, intensively managed sanctuaries, it costs $1200 per annum, a significant proportion of South Africa's national park budget of $79 million. This funding is under pressure as the new South Africa deals with more pressing demands, such as spiralling crime and widespread poverty.

It was against this background that in 1994 CITES recognized the need for rhino range states to develop innovative means for generating income to cover shortfalls in conservation funding. Trading in live animals was permitted by CITES for just this reason. Trading in rhino products is the logical extension of this thinking.

In their proposal, the South Africans explain that 76 per cent of the white rhino population is managed by their national parks. These parks would reinvest the revenues from rhino products into conservation programmes. The sustainable use of white rhino through live sales and sport hunting has already contributed $2 million to rhino conservation. According to wildlife economist, Michael 't Sas Rolfes, South Africa could sustainably supply the Far East market with one tonne of rhino horn a year and potentially generate a further $2 million.

Animal-rights activists oppose the idea. They argue, and the USA agrees, that legalization will encourage poaching because international trade will be difficult, if not impossible, to monitor as officials will not be able to discern legal horns from illegal ones.

But South Africa is proposing a high-tech tracking device to tackle this problem. All horns contain trace elements that are unique to the specific location from which the rhino originated. Cheap and reliable scientific tests can pinpoint the area of origin.

Such ideas have done little to sway animal-rights activists. Groups like HSUS and the London-based International Fund for Animal Welfare want to maintain an absolute ban and are relying on the usual arsenal of shock tactics that have brought them success in the past. They like to show alarming pictures of wildlife killings, but the tactic misrepresents isolated incidents as wholesale slaughter.

Journalists tend to take the activists at their word, despite the fact that they often get their fingers burnt. In 1995 Greenpeace-doctored data incorrectly claimed that Shell Oil's North Sea *Brent Spar* oil platform contained high amounts of toxic waste that would pollute the marine environment. More recently, the HSUS reported that 8000 endangered Botswanan porcupines had been imported into the USA when in fact 8000 porcupine quills had been imported.

Any politician, corporation or analyst who questions the data risks an assault in the media mounted by the politically correct activists. But the tables may be about to turn. At the CITES meeting, the politically correct animal-rights activists will face off against the equally politically correct black rural communities of South Africa.

Normally, voting governments with no vested interest in a species find it politically expedient to concede to the demands of animal-rights organizations. But now the communities are fighting back. They have joined forces with local conservation groups to lobby CITES and address common misunderstandings about conservation. According to Jon Hutton, Director of the Africa Resources Trust in Harare, Zimbabwe: 'Not only has international trade never driven a species to extinction, but only rarely has it ever been a major contributory factor. The principal cause of extinction, we now know, is the introduction of alien species to islands, followed by habitat loss and then hunting, primarily for food, while international trade ranks a distant fourth'.

According to Dr Hutton, the future of Africa's wild species depends on the goodwill of the rural people who have to share their land and water with these animals and plants. Conservation-based community development programmes offer hope for the coexistence of wildlife and rural people, provided that these communities gain access to a full range of revenue-generating options. Otherwise they will be forced to displace or destroy their wildlife to improve their quality of life.

The case for trade in rhino products is watertight. If CITES does not approve these initiatives, thus limiting future funding for conservation, it will indirectly be helping to kill off rhinos.

58 Don't demonize technology

Wall Street Journal Europe (28 July 1997)

Modern life is dependent on technology. Gasoline engines have made travel possible for most, pesticides have drastically reduced food prices, and medicine has eradicated many infectious diseases in the developed world.

But as Edward Tenner eloquently explains in his often entertaining book, *Why Things Bite Back: New Technology and the Revenge Effect* (Fourth Estate, 1996), each of these advances has spawned a 'revenge effect' in which the solution to one problem leads to other, unforeseen, problems. The Princeton University historian, however, comes out, on balance, in favour of technology, sending an important message to the neo-Luddites and environmentalists who revel in publicizing the unfortunate side-effects of progress.

Tenner illustrates his argument with wide-ranging and well-researched case studies. Animals introduced to alien countries with the best of intentions, for example, have often become serious pests. The weasel-like stoat, brought to New Zealand last century to control rabbits, devastated native birds. The African killer bee, introduced to the USA in the 1960s to boost honey production, has killed several Americans. Antibiotics, which have rid the Western world of infectious diseases like cholera, have given rise to resistant bacteria. Air travel has allowed viruses to spread like wildfire. Indeed, wild fires are now more severe because fire suppression methods allow tinder to build up on forest floors. Tenner also outlines many examples of government agencies promoting a technology or product, only to spend money eradicating it later. The most famous government-inspired revenge effect is that of the pesticide DDT. It's widely acknowledged that DDT spraying rid large areas of Asia and Africa of insect-borne diseases such as typhus and malaria, saving millions of lives. Moreover, DDT replaced older, extremely toxic, arsenic-based pesticides and increased agricultural productivity in the process.

But DDT was so effective and resilient as a pesticide that it accumulated in the tissue of living organisms. Studies showed that the higher the animal was on the food chain, the more DDT remained in its system, affecting reproduction and killing off predators, especially eagles. After a decade or so, other effects emerged. DDT led to serious pest infestation, as it was often more effective at killing off the larger insects that fed on the pests themselves. Pests also developed resistance to DDT's effects, and it was being phased out for this reason when the international outcry against it began.

Governments should examine the potential downsides of new technologies in their licensing processes. But as Tenner and many environmentalists point out, adverse effects may not emerge until the new technology is in use. Radical environmental groups like Greenpeace use this fear of the unknown to protest against the introduction of technological advances such as new pesticides, raising the spectre of human cancer and reduced fertility.

But, as Tenner subtly acknowledges, even following the 'safe' route suggested by some environmentalists produces risks and costs. Modern pesticides are far more efficient and environment-friendly than DDT, and like DDT are non-toxic to humans. The science journal *Nature* recently concluded that DDT poses a negligible risk to humans, and that pushing for a ban of pesticides (even DDT) would be self-defeating because at least a million people die of mosquito-transmitted malaria every year. Reducing the use of pesticides would also lead to more crop failures and higher food prices. And for most people in the world, poor diet is a far greater and more immediate health hazard than ingesting pesticide residues.

As technological advances continue to appear at a seemingly exponential rate, maintaining a perspective on their relative costs and benefits will be critical. Tenner's conclusion – that new technologies require vigilance, not demonization or banishment – is a useful contribution to the debate.

59 Fear and precaution: A lethal mix?

Economist (21 August 1998) and *Financial Times* (14 August 1998)

Survey after survey shows that some people worry so much about the future that they believe that new technologies and products should not be permitted until it is known for certain they won't endanger health and environment. Precaution has become the cry of risk averse activists and ambitious politicians eager to make a name appeasing them.

I recently tried mild ridicule to attack this modern urge to 'banish by survey' by conducting my own survey about whether water (called dihydrogen monoxide or DHMO in the survey) should be banned by the EU. My survey explained that DHMO had many nasty effects such as contributing to acid rain and being a constituent in cancerous cells. Despite the extravagant claims of harm, very few got the joke, and 76 per cent of Londoners thought water should be banned.

It has been gratifying to have reports flood in from academic departments around Europe with results similar to my own. London University geographers scored a mind numbing 86 per cent, whereas German economists did best at 40 per cent, perhaps because many economists are cynics, and assumed correctly that there was something fishy about the survey. The UK Science Minister, John Battle, even used the survey result in his speech to the annual UK Chemical Industry Association Dinner, to make the point that a true fact (water is found in cancerous cells) can lead some people who are scientifically illiterate to make a false conclusion (water is dangerous). However, the survey had a more subtle counter-intuitive aim, which was to

…at even a substance required by every living creature can be …ous. Of course, to ingest a fatal amount of water is very difficult, unless …rowns, but it is possible.

A more obvious example of substances essential at low doses but poisonous at high doses are vitamins. For example, it would be relatively easy to poison oneself on vitamin A, but one could not live without a small amount of it.

The notion that the dose makes the poison has been known for centuries but seems to be forgotten in modern health and environmental regulation. I recently edited a book (*What Risk?*, 1997) with the explicit aim of showing that modern regulations are based on the erroneous assumption that because something is dangerous at high doses it also causes harm at low doses. As the numerous experts in *What Risk?* demonstrate there is a threshold below which the defence mechanisms and metabolic processes of human beings can cope perfectly well. For example, there are nineteen known carcinogens in coffee, yet normal consumption is not a concern. However, if coffee were discovered today it would probably be banned by some health agencies, since coffee provides worse test results than many banned synthetic chemicals.

When the basis for much current regulation was laid some forty years ago, the science was insufficiently clear to show whether there were safe thresholds for modern carcinogens. Today, the evidence shows that safe thresholds exist, yet the policies remain based on the old science.

When regulators are confronted with this evidence their response is often to say, 'At least we are reducing some risks'. However, every attempt to reduce risk involves a trade-off, and concentrating on minuscule risks may increase our exposure to more real threats.

As a society, we must focus on big risks before small ones and always look at the trade-offs involved when a pressure group or politician demands that we banish a product or a process. Of course, new technologies bring new hazards, but they usually replace older technologies which were more harmful. Prudent use and monitoring of new technologies, and not banishment of them, will continue to lower, but never eliminate, risk.

60 The origins of virtue

Economic Affairs (September 1998)

The Origins of Virtue (Matt Ridley, 1997, Penguin) was, without doubt, the most informative book I read in 1997, with huge implications for public policy. Ridley explains with great clarity how we practise what he calls 'reciprocal altruism' in our social interactions. We are nice to each other until we are given reason not to be, when we ostracize those who break the social contract.

Ridley is the foremost science writer in Britain today. Boasting an Oxford University PhD in zoology, several books on evolution and a former American editorship of *The Economist,* Ridley is uniquely qualified to tackle the paradox of selfishness leading to cooperation. But not only does Ridley explain this paradox, he does so in a refreshingly clear and readable style.

Free-market economists realized the importance of Dawkins' *Selfish Gene* (Oxford Paperbacks, 1989) as it enabled them to explain human actions as rational that otherwise appeared altruistic. Why else would old people leave money to their children, rather than just spend it on entertainment or monuments to themselves? As Ridley puts it 'the money is following the genes, even if it abandons the individuals'. However, Ridley goes further than Dawkins.

While Ridley makes an academic study of human behaviour and human institutions, he understands the significance of his research to modern public policy. 'Markets, exchanges and rules develop before government. Because they have been part of human nature for millions of years', he claims. But his analysis takes us further than the spontaneous economic order of philosophers like Hayek. He condemns governments as the cause of the disintegration of societal norms, which serve little purpose other than benefiting special interest groups and the governmental bureaucracy itself.

Beginning with the philosophy of Hobbes and Rousseau, Matt Ridley traces the evolution of society, first among genes, then among cells, then in ants, bats, apes, dolphins and finally, among human beings. Ridley draws on game theory – the simplified mathematical representation of reality – to explain that in one-off situations 'selfish' actions make sense, but in recurring situations, as in real life, cooperation is best. He gives numerous examples of self-interest in the animal kingdom leading to cooperation.

For instance, a grouper fish, finding a shoal of small fish hovering around a reef, opens its mouth, not to eat them, which it easily could, but to let them swim in its mouth and clean off debris around its gills. The grouper has come to a cleaning station, long established in a particular spot, and visited by many customers to the mutual benefit of all – the cleaner fish have their food brought to them in return for their services to the larger fish.

However, humans have taken cooperation infinitely further than even community animals like bees and insects. We are equipped with predispositions to learn how to cooperate, to discriminate the trustworthy from the treacherous, to commit ourselves to be trustworthy, to earn good reputations, to exchange goods and information and to divide labour.

For example, a highly efficient and homogeneous law was developed in the mid-twelfth century among English and Venetian merchants which gave them substantial protection in trading disputes all over Europe. Merchant law, based on good customs and methods of settlement, was practised in formal courts, whose strongest deterrent was social ostracism and exclusion 'hey were considered superior to royal and state courts in their ringing them to the attention of governments. According to

> go...nents had not even woken up to what was going on. An entirely private, voluntary and informal system of exchange had developed. In a flurry government began to act. It enacted into national laws these merchant customs, allowed appeals to royal courts – and of course took the credit. Henry II of England was not a great law giver, he was a great law nationaliser.

And so it has been in other areas of life. Human coordination has solved many problems, only for the solutions to be nationalized, where cooperation is replaced by coercion. Coercion and nationalization often lead to failure and vastly increased costs. Ridley concludes that many social, environmental and, of course, economic problems are the fault of government. The collapse of community spirit in the last few decades, and the erosion of civic virtue, are caused not by the spread and encouragement of greed but by the dead hand of Leviathan. 'The state makes no bargain with the citizen to take joint responsibility for civic order, engenders in him no obligation, duty or pride, and imposes obedience instead. Little wonder that, treated like a naughty child, he behaves like one', he writes.

His book is far more than a warning against the encroaching Leviathan, it is a treatise on trust and openness. 'Trust everyone unless you have a reason not to', is the motto of Lord Vinson, a successful British entrepreneur, who Ridley cites. It is a rule for life, and one that would serve anyone well. This is a marvellous book, and I cannot recommend it highly enough.

61 Trial and error is better than trial without error

Accountancy Magazine (October 1998)

These days the surest sign that a society is affluent is its susceptibility to scares. By every objective measure, such as infant mortality and life expectancy, the British are healthier today and exposed to fewer and lesser hazards than ever in our history. Yet, because we live longer and have more leisure time, we have the luxury of contemplating those remaining hazards.

Environmental organizations, using Germanic philosophy, have fed on this concern and have promoted a particular interpretation of the Treaty of Rome's precautionary principle. This is a proposition that new technologies and products should not be permitted until we know they won't endanger health and environment. The principle has become the categorical imperative of environmentalists: thou shalt not tolerate even the risk of a risk.

A good illustration of the precautionary principle at work is the debate on pesticides. Many environmentalists point out that the adverse effects of a pesticide such as DDT did not emerge until years after it was first used. Although not harmful to humans, it accumulated up the food chain until it affected carnivorous predators such as otters and eagles. Because we did not foresee this problem, they argue, we should ban today's pesticides whose effects tomorrow we also cannot predict. Indeed, Danish environmental officials, under constant lobbying from their powerful environment movement, are currently discussing a ban on all pesticides.

However, it should be remembered that DDT was cheap to produce and replaced older arsenic-based pesticides, which were fatal to humans and toxic to the environment; it also rid America, Europe and large parts of Africa and Asia of mosquito-borne diseases such as malaria and typhus. DDT lies unused in less developed countries as a result of adopting the Western perception of risk, while the World Health Organisation reports that malaria is on the increase, killing 2 million people a year worldwide. Importantly, the effects of DDT have been reversible: otter and eagle populations have recovered. And, as we learn more, so products become more benign. The replacements for DDT were far less harmful to the environment if not to humans.

According to Bruce Ames, Professor of Biochemistry at the University of California, Berkeley, without pesticides there would be pressure to cultivate more land, potentially reducing biodiversity and, crucially, food would be much more expensive. A poor diet (low in pesticide-protected fruits and vegetables) is a far greater and more immediate health hazard than ingesting pesticide residues ever could be, and the poor would suffer most from dearer fresh produce. Therefore, he concludes that 'the risk from using pesticides is far lower than the risk from not using them'.

This balancing act cuts no ice with the environmentalists. All that appears to matter to activists is whether a substance or technology may do harm. The campaign against genetic research for the bio-food markets bears these hallmarks. According to the green precautionary position, foods such as melons and maize genetically modified to resist pests may have indefinable and irreversible consequences on ecosystems. Most scientists accept that there is a tiny risk of altered genes reaching the environment, and that a tiny percentage of these could be harmful. However, genetically-altered crops need less pesticide as they are resistant to many pests. So advances in biotechnology should please environmentalists for reducing the perceived dangers from pesticides. Yet they seem reluctant to acknowledge this silver lining to the biotech cloud.

The public, on the other hand, do acknowledge this trade-off. In a recent study, Richard Braun, professor of microbiology at the University of Berne, Switzerland, showed that Swiss public acceptance for genetically-modified maize was very low until it was pointed out that fewer pesticides would be used on modified maize than on conventional maize. The unknown risks of genetic manipulation were being compared with the perceived risks of pesticide use and, under these circumstances, the public were happier to accept the new technology along with the possibility of irreversible harm, rather than pay a high price for not having that technology.

In essence, there are no absolutes: risk is relative. Some hazards are more dangerous than others, so governments should attempt to reduce major risks before tackling minor ones. Unfortunately, using the precautionary principle often means regulations are targeted at minor hazards. For example, bans on certain chemicals may not cost a regulatory agency anything but will probably have a cost in terms of increased product prices. As Professor Kip Viscusi from Harvard University has shown in *Risks, Costs and Lives Saved* (American Enterprise Institute, 1996) the more of the regulatory budget spent on banning pesticide use and removing them from public water supplies, the less that can be spent on resources that have a better return in lives saved, such as road safety. The US government demands for more fuel-efficient cars have forced makers to make light cars that are more dangerous if crashed. Bob Crandall of the independent Brookings Institute says, 'at least 3000 people die every year because of fuel economy standards'. The opportunity costs are obvious. Regulations that cost more than they save should be scrapped.

However, Green claims of precaution and demands for government regulation of specific products are rarely challenged. This is because lobbied regulators are often only responsible for harms from specific technologies (the minute possibility of death from pesticide ingestion) and they may not see (or won't be responsible for) the bigger picture (the resultant higher rates of cancer from lower intake of pesticide-protected fruits and vegetables, due to higher food prices). Therefore, Green lobbying often results in harmful regulation. There is little doubt that if Prometheus discovered fire tomorrow, it would be banned by an overzealous health and safety agency.

62 Allocating water: By market or bureaucracy?

Economic Affairs (December 1998)

It was fashionable a few years ago to believe that future wars, especially in the Middle East, would be fought over water. Commentators nodded sagely when the chair of the 1992 UN Water Conference in Dublin described the 'profligate waste and degradation that has resulted from the neglect of effective water resources management'. Since then many high profile conferences have come and gone, but little progress has been made as water conflicts abound at the local, regional and international levels. But in early July, a water conference at the University in Aix-en-Provence laid the intellectual foundations of a solution to these problems, even though it had none of the usual razzmatazz of such events, and no high-level political leaders were in attendance.

The French water system's relatively decentralized administered pricing system is admired by many in the world's multilateral agencies such as the UN Development Programme and is promoted by many academics. It is seen as effectual and simple to administer. In fact, as a model it has only one major competitor – allocation of water by the market. Markets in water have evolved in many countries, notably the USA, Chile and Mexico. Advocates include many experts at the World Bank and water specialists, such as Professor Terry Anderson of the Montana-based think tank; the Political Economy Research Center.

The two schools of thought have had little time for each other before. The French school considers water a special case, so that equitable allocation of water by the market is impossible. The market school sees political allocation as inefficient, with allocation favouring the politically powerful, whereas the market allocates water more efficiently and often more fairly. At the Aix-en-Provence conference the two schools were brought together by organizer Max Falque, to discuss the similarities and differences of their approaches.

Professor Barbara Pozzo from Milan University explained that the systems derived from different legal histories, the market system based on Anglo-American common law and the French/Continental system based upon the Napoleonic code. One of the key problems for analysis was the semantics used in the different traditions and hence consensus did not look possible from the early discussions. Jean-Paul Chirouze, Director of the Rhône-Mediterranean regional water agency, claimed the success of the 'preparation of a master plan for each river basin by local administrators' where stakeholders had an input to allocation. He claimed that market allocation would benefit the large players and would ignore more diverse stakeholders. Professor Anderson discussed regulatory capture by powerful stakeholders, such as farmers. He explained how markets save people from the chronic water scarcity that regulatory capture caused, 'by removing planning control from administrators and replacing it with the discipline of the market'.

Despite the rhetoric, the similarities were greater than the differences. Most of the participants that I spoke to thought that the key elements to a successful water system were: local control of water resources, including monitoring and enforcement of water use; flexibility to allow for changes in demand; and the reduction of subsidies to supply augmentation for agriculture (which still uses 73 per cent of water worldwide). Professor William Blomquist of Indiana University explained how locally administered systems and water-market systems are almost identical in the rules under which decisions are made, the only difference is that individual exchanges are not allowed in the former.

Professor Blomquist favoured a local, communal-property system, where internal rights to use water could be traded within the community, a key advantage being that this system would react to changes in demand faster than even an efficient bureaucracy. Blomquist's compromise seemed attractive to many of the participants on both sides of the debate. Indeed, it showed that the key enemy to both schools of thought is centralization of water control and over interference by government. Apart from setting environmental and equity requirements most parties agreed that the government should have a limited role to play in water allocation.

However, while the participators were largely optimistic, they realized that the time for change is today. Many countries of the world are following vicious circles of water control. Centralized management leads to inefficient and inequitable use, which leads to further governmental control. As populations expand, decentralized control (preferably with local markets) will become more essential, but less politically likely as governments will need to be seen to be doing something. Breaking that vicious circle is important for most countries of the world, for political hot spots like the Middle East it is essential.

63 Culling to be kind

On Point (April 1999) (see www.cei.org, www.iea.org.uk)

Next week nearly 34 tonnes of elephant ivory from Namibia and Zimbabwe will be shipped to Japan. The sale, agreed in principle nineteen months ago and worth $5 million, was enabled by the partial overturn of a 1989 ban on international ivory trade. This is good news for both the environment and the people of Africa. But last month, plans were discovered of a US animal rights group using evidence gathered secretly by South African anti-poaching police to discredit the trade and campaign for a halt on future sales.

Southern African countries have made a meticulous case for resuming trade in ivory (albeit on a restricted basis), against opposition from certain international interest groups, who have expressed concern that the ivory trade would encourage uncontrolled elephant slaughter. George Hughes, head of the Natal Parks Board in South Africa, and many others like him, have convinced most trade sceptics that the ban, agreed under the auspices of the UN Convention on International Trade in Endangered Species (CITES), should be lifted. At the CITES meeting in Harare in Zimbabwe in July 1997 a majority of signatory nations voted in favour of a limited resumption of ivory trading. However, the two-thirds majority required for lifting the ban was only just reached and since the USA, the UK and many influential northern countries either abstained or voted against, the pro-trade position is still precarious.

Nevertheless, all the evidence suggests that regulated ivory trade is sustainable, provides much-needed revenue directly to local communities and is environmentally beneficial. Sound resource management necessitates elephant culling in order to conserve other species, whilst if local people are able to benefit from the revenue they have stronger incentives to conserve stocks for the future. In addition, the ivory market in Japan is very stable. 20,000 retail outlets sell hankos, popular signature seals given to boys to mark the beginning of manhood. Plastic imitations will not do, so this demand will be constant, providing certainty to African sellers. Also, ivory stockpiles are being used up and the hankos market is hungry for supplies; without legal trade illegal sources would probably be sought.

Militant animal rights groups such as the US-based International Fund for Animal Welfare (IFAW) have previously sabotaged pro-trade efforts using alarmist propaganda but this time they are even subverting the role of government departments. IFAW can't stop next week's ivory sale but by planning a media hit purporting to show, in almost pornographic detail, fresh evidence of poaching, apparently from reputable government sources, they aim to make the trade to Japan a one-off – an aberration in an otherwise decade-long ban.

Peter Mokaba, South Africa's Deputy Environment Minister, last month called for an investigation into the actions of the South African Endangered Species Protection Unit (ESPU) – a police unit specially designed to fight poaching. Last year the cash-strapped ESPU secretly accepted $460,000 from IFAW. According to Mokaba, the money was ostensibly for staff training but was actually spent on gathering data on ivory poaching across Africa that IFAW will employ in their proposed smear campaign. No one, Mokaba included, is opposed to gathering data on poaching incidents, but 'the ESPU did not disclose their whole intention to South Africa or other African countries,' said Mokaba. Ministers were unaware of the donation and it has become an embarrassment to them.

Chris Styles, deputy director of the South African Rhino and Elephant Foundation resigned as advisor to IFAW protesting 'the political ramifications' of IFAW's funding tactics. He was particularly concerned that ESPU could be 'contracted' to do an investigation for the foreign pressure group.

ESPU's Project Jumbo gathered data on poaching incidents across Africa, and involved 242 man-days of field research. The draft report, not publicly released, has strong animal rights overtones, claiming poaching to be 'deviant behaviour', even equating it to rape.

Such rhetoric is unusual for a police unit and what is more, given the time spent gathering evidence, the report is thin on detail. While the most obvious conclusion of this report is that poaching is reasonably well under control, it is expected by insiders that the most lurid incidents have been held back from publication and will be presented by IFAW prior to the ivory trade to Japan. Isolated poaching incidents are likely to be blown out of all proportion to support IFAW's claim that re-opening trade encourages poaching.

IFAW's thesis is that any legal trade will be used to provide cover for massive illegal trade because ivory in transit will not automatically be seen as illegally shipped, and hence will not be confiscated.

There is no doubt that re-opening trade makes monitoring of illegal trades slightly harder. However, security measures demanded by CITES and implemented by Zimbabwe, Namibia and Japan have been well designed and, crucially for the former two countries, can be well executed with funds released from trade.

International trade issues attract media coverage and appeal to fund-raisers in animal rights organizations but trade and poaching are not the elephant's main problem. Growing human populations means that elephants must more and more compete with Africa's smallholder farmers for living space. Farmers kill elephants whenever possible because they trample their crops and destroy villages. This is the key reason why elephant numbers have declined in places such as Kenya and Tanzania. Nevertheless, the elephant is far from endangered with well over 500,000 animals across Africa.

Perversely, the 1989 trade ban allowed poaching to increase in some Southern African countries because funds previously received from ivory sales were no longer available to pay for anti-poaching units. Making elephants valuable to Africans by allowing them to own the animals and trade in their products is the best way to ensure the species' sustained existence. Zimbabwe has done this most effectively and now villagers love their elephants as looking after them brings good returns alongside farming and other rural employment possibilities. Zimbabwean farmers, unlike their northern counterparts, do not turn a blind eye to poaching. It was precisely because of these arguments that trade is resuming.

Environment Minister Mokaba echoes the concerns of wildlife experts that the ESPU investigation is 'part of a broader picture' to undermine the gains made at the Harare CITES meeting in 1997.

The decision taken at Harare to 'downlist' elephant populations to allow trade from Southern African nations was seen by many as the first step in re-opening trade throughout Africa. But Mokaba contends that ESPU has been misused to undermine the possibility of expanding trade. It is likely that the 12 countries involved in Project Jumbo supplied sensitive security information to the ESPU, thinking it was for government eyes only. Instead, wildlife experts fear the information may have been passed to one of the most vociferous animal rights opponents.

Piet Lategan, head of ESPU, denies that public funds or the ESPU have been misused and it is reported that he would welcome 'any investigation by anyone'. Minister Mokaba, reportedly livid at ESPU actions, may yet oblige him.

Poaching will continue across Africa, as poor Africans look for ways to make ends meet. But this poaching will not predominate in Southern African countries, because hunting rights (and soon ivory sales) deliver funds to protect animals. In the coming days it is likely that poaching incidents, allegedly escalating because of the resumption of trade, will make news headlines.

Western media have been spoon-fed photomontage stories before by pressure groups. Consider the BBC airing of Greenpeace-doctored video footage of Shell's Brent Spar Oil platform. It would be a tragedy if after 10 years' effort to lift a counterproductive ban, ivory trade is threatened because of western governmental pressure on CITES, caused by media representations of poaching pornography. Although legal ivory trade involves the death of a particular elephant, it may be the surest way to protect the species.

Environmentalists claim that illegal wildlife trade is globally second only to the drug trade in value, perhaps being worth more than $5bn annually. It is time to take the money away from the criminals and give it to the Africans who look after the animals.

64 Speechless in Seattle

Novo Magazine (December 1999)

As the protestors, delegates, and tear gas disperse from the recent Seattle World Trade Organization (WTO) meeting, the more interesting but less newsworthy conflicts are emerging. These conflicts will not have an effect on proceedings, since the media did not report them, but they explain more about the nature of the problem at Seattle than most others. For what emerged is that the protestors are the new third way fascists: they are not interested in debate; they don't want to hear other opinions; they only want control. And it looks more and more that their saner elements will be granted access to the WTO in the future – an unappetizing prospect.

In a week of incoherent protests outside the WTO meeting one public debate, on the crossroads of Pike St and University St in downtown Seattle, stood out as unique. Representatives of the only genuinely pro free trade non-governmental organization, the International Consumers for Civil Society, were attempting to debate the green protectionists who were preventing delegates from attending the meeting.

Barun Mitra, ICCS member and managing trustee of the New Delhi-based Liberty Institute, asked protestors, ranging from grunge-dressed civil disobedience types to the more aggressive balaclava-adorned nihilists, why they would not let him pass. The response was a panoply of placards and chants – 'Say No to WTO', 'People Before Profits', 'Fair Trade Not Free Trade', were the most common. More specific messages involved opposition to genetically modified foods, and especially the multinationals behind the commercialisation of the science of biotechnology. Mr Mitra tried to understand their concerns, but pointed out that farmers in his country wanted vitamin A enhanced genetically modified rice to overcome widespread blindness from poor diets. The protestors just shouted louder and continued with the 'You're a Capitalist Pig' and 'We Hate Corporate Greed' abuse.

Another ICCS delegate, Fran Smith explained how consumers benefited from free trade, including cheaper cameras from the far east, with which many of the demonstrators were adorned. No doubt this infuriated the rapidly developing mob even more and Mrs Smith told me afterwards she felt very threatened by the encircling of the young men hurling vitriolic threats. The questioning of ideals by Mr Mitra and Mrs Smith with the anti-WTO protestors was cut short by the tear gassing of protestors a block upwind, and as the gas floated down, talking and seeing became difficult and then impossible. This was a pity, since it was the only substantive debate occurring outside of the Ministerial Convention Center all week.

The local television networks claimed that half the protestors were from the local area and especially the University of Washington and local Seattle high schools, nearly all of whom could not imagine what it must be like to be a poor farmer in rural India. And its people like Mr Mitra's farming friends that further open trade would help.

Andrew Crosby from the British NGO the International Centre for Trade and Sustainable Development, explained to me why there were so many protestors afforded the possibility of being in Seattle. Because of the strength of the Wall Street Stock Market over the past year, the numerous foundations established by wealthy American entrepreneurs have had to disburse funds to their selected worthy causes in larger amounts, and hence faster, than normal. 'Much of this considerable wealth has ended up in the hands of protesting NGOs' confirmed Mr Crosby, who was one of many peaceful NGO delegates to the WTO. Its an interesting irony that wealth created through open trade is being used to support mainly inarticulate protests against it. Indeed, most of those that I spoke to on the barricades in Seattle had no idea what they were protesting against.

Effectively, the protestors were denying developing countries access to the benefits of free trade, and for a while were completely successful. On the first day, demonstrators blocked the road to the convention centre with a sit-down protest. Police managed to cordon an area around the centre and the nearby hotels. Unfortunately, many of the poorer and less well-organized, like me and the entire Nigerian delegation, were staying several miles away, and simply could not break through the protest. We came a long way not to have a say. That same evening in a piece of classic hypocrisy, a young hooligan was seen trashing the 'Nike Center' – ostensibly because of child labour accusations – while wearing a pair of Nike trainers. His fashion sense must have overcome or preceded his humanitarian conviction, if that is what made him attack the store.

The protestors certainly stopped trade in Seattle, since the only flourishing trade all week was in bottled water to overcome the tear gas, and in spray paints for graffiti. This would only have mattered to the numerous traders of Seattle, but its reach may have been far wider. US President Clinton in a pathetic attempt to placate US labour unions (supporting Al Gore's Presidential campaign) suggested in a speech the day after the major riots, that labour rights be brought into the negotiations. The developing world sees labour standards as covert western protection, and so agreement foundered. They know that the real choice facing a 12-year-old farm worker in China or India is not between school or 'exploitation', but between knowing he and his family can eat tomorrow and not knowing. Whether Clinton changed his speech because of the rioters is hard to say, but if so, then they can rightly claim that they 'Stopped the WTO'. Personally, I can't see what triumph there is in that. Time will tell whether the WTO can let the developing countries come to the world fair, but while such outspoken ignorance has influence it seems increasingly unlikely.

It was odd for me to be defending the WTO in Seattle since I think its agreements are based on a false premise – that a country's leaders should only open markets for reciprocal trade. The true benefits of free trade mainly accrue to consumers because they get a better deal due to greater choice and hence competition. A country benefits hugely from being able to buy from all other countries even if it cannot export into all those countries. However, the mercantilist basis of the WTO has served us all well over the past 50 years by opening up markets and encouraging a massive increase in international trade and the wealth this generates. Perhaps the WTO needs to stress the benefits to consumers of free trade – this would explain why so many of the world's economists think trade is such a good idea. Its not because MacDonalds can sell hamburgers in the Far East but that we can import cheaper fruit from Chile and South Africa in winter. But most of all free trade helps developing countries export raw materials and low valued goods to sell to rich countries. It starts them on a virtuous circle, and not a vicious circle, which most of the WTO protests, if successful, will condemn them to.

65 Earth Report 2000

Wall Street Journal (23 December 1999)

According to the French mathematician and philosopher Blaise Pascal, our first moral obligation is to think clearly. With his introduction to *Earth Report 2000*, theologian Michael Novak reminds us of Pascal's dictum, and sets the tone for an impressive and clear thinking book. *Earth Report 2000* (Bailey ed., McGraw Hill), a collection of papers by experts in fields relevant to environmental thought, explains why we are not heading towards environmental Armageddon, while policies designed by bureaucrats to save us are more likely to harm us. Stephen Safe, Professor of Toxicology at Texas A&M University, Dr Roy Spencer from NASA, and Harvard's Nicholas Eberstadt are just three of the experts who remind us in their chapters that things are, on the whole, getting better. The final chapter of the book is a collection of over 30 environmental benchmarks collated by staff of the Washington DC think tank, the Competitive Enterprise Institute. Nearly all these measures, from air and water quality to energy efficiency, have improved in recent decades, which neatly exposes the unfounded doom and gloom of environmental reporters. Since the book is predominantly optimistic, it should not come as a surprise to find that it is dedicated to the memory of the arch clear thinker and renowned optimist, Julian Simon.

Simon used to enthuse, almost uniquely, that population growth was good for the planet, because for each mouth that had to be fed came a brain and two hands with which to think and work. But far from a population explosion Eberstadt shows that 79 countries have reproductive rates too low to replace current population levels, numerous other countries have decelerating growth rates (soon to fall below replacement level). One is left with the impression that Simon would be concerned that there were not going to be enough people in the new millennium.

Editor Ronald Bailey's chapter 'The progress explosion: permanently escaping the Malthusian trap' furthers our understanding of the Simon thesis that human ingenuity and desires have always overcome pressures of larger populations. Arguments that higher agricultural production will simply lead to more people, putting more pressure on ecosystems, are dismissed by Bailey. He amusingly explains that for developed countries 'more food doesn't mean more children, it means more fat, old people'. Bailey also exposes the malign effects of certain neo-Malthusians who, for example, try to deny oral rehydration therapy to young children in developing countries because they might grow up into poverty and possible starvation.

Perhaps the most controversial chapter is written by Indur Goklany of the US Department of the Interior. Along with NASA's Spencer he explains why only very limited global warming is ever likely, given negative feed-backs in our environment (such as increasing carbon dioxide absorption by plants as atmospheric concentrations rise). Furthermore, the idea that we in the North will be inundated with malaria and infectious diseases as temperatures rise is shown to be folly. Alleviating these problems can be addressed far more effectively and cheaply with methods, such as pesticide spraying, other than reducing carbon emissions. In short, Goklany exposes the UN's Kyoto Climate Protocol as pointless: it would reduce temperatures at most by 0.07°C, and that adaptation to climate change (which will occur naturally anyway) is a cheaper and more sensible option for developed and especially developing countries.

Other chapters on wildlife management and energy policies are interesting but not particularly controversial, the chapter on fisheries is the only depressing one in the book. Fish stocks are depleting quickly in many areas because of inappropriate institutional structures. There is no clear ownership (and hence stewardship) of the oceans, and without this, the world's fishermen race to catch fish, inevitably depleting stocks. Only in the seas controlled by New Zealand and Iceland, where a tradable quota (i.e. the market) has operated have stocks recovered and profits risen. Privatizing the seas would undoubtedly save the fish in them, but does not appear to be a solution favourable to the world's politicians.

Having lost the scientific arguments that ambient levels of synthetic chemicals cause cancer, the Greens' latest anxiety campaign has been that these same chemicals cause hormonal and reproductive problems in humans. Professor Safe explains that at most their claims are overplayed, at worst completely unfounded. Sperm counts are probably not falling and if they are there is no evidence it has anything to do with modern chemicals. Furthermore, the estrogenic (feminizing) effects of synthetics, such as from pesticides like DDT, do exist but are dwarfed (by several thousand times) by naturally-occurring estrogen-mimicking substances in our food. The only synthetic substance that has a major effect on reproduction is ethynyl estradiol. But that should come as no surprise, since it is the main ingredient in the contraceptive pill. In short, the Greens have targeted substances they don't like rather than those most likely to have an effect.

In fact, the book taken as a whole shows the mendacity of the green lobby. Their forecasts of impending disaster may be good for fund raising but have led to poor environmental policies and slowed economic growth, which has harmed the very people they say they want to help – in the developing world. *Earth Report 2000* is an antidote to all this alarmism, it should be read by all those interested in the fate of our planet in the next century.

Index

JULIAN MORRIS • ROGER BATE
FEARING FOOD
RISK, HEALTH & ENVIRONMENT
BH